Working from Home
on the internet

A practical guide to increasing
your income by working online

Laurel Alexander
MIPD MICG

www.internet-handbooks.co.uk

Other Internet Handbooks by the same author

Careers Guidance on the Internet
Education & Training on the Internet
Graduate Job Hunting on the Internet
Human Resource Management on the Internet
Overseas Job Hunting on the Internet

First published in 2001 by Internet Handbooks Ltd, Plymbridge House, Estover Road, Plymouth PL6 7PY, United Kingdom.

Customer services tel:	(01752) 202301
Orders fax:	(01752) 202333
Customer services email:	cservs@plymbridge.com
Distributors web site:	http://www.plymbridge.com
Internet Handbooks web site:	http://www.internet-handbooks.co.uk

Note: The contents of this book are offered for the purposes of general guidance only and no liability can be accepted for any loss or expense incurred as a result of relying in particular circumstances on statements made in this book. Readers are advised to check the current position with the appropriate authorities before entering into personal arrangements.

Case studies in this book are entirely fictional and any resemblance to real persons or organisations is entirely coincidental.

Printed and bound by The Cromwell Press Ltd, Trowbridge, Wiltshire.

Contents

Contents..

List of illustrations

· ·

Illustrations..

Preface

Working from home using the internet? – and making money? Is it possible?

Earning money from technology isn't new. Word processing, desktop publishing (DTP) and direct mail for example have been around for a long while. But the internet – that's something else. You can now earn money through having your own web site and using it to sell a product or service. You can also make money through other people's web sites. You can make money simply by surfing the web. You can make money through conducting research on the web. You can make money by being employed by someone else, and using technology and internet facilities. You can make money through helping other people to make money through the web. There are a thousand opportunities and business ideas to exploit, and almost endless permutations of ideas and techniques. You could acquire ten different employers or clients scattered over the globe and never have to commute! You can sit at home anywhere in the world, log onto the internet and enjoy an international perspective on your monitor. And of course the internet now offers a global marketplace in which you can sell.

Homeworking has sometimes had a negative image of exploited people doing menial jobs for a pittance. Indeed, this does happen. However, many thousands of businessmen and women do run successful and profitable businesses from home, in some cases making a very large amount of money. There are several good books on the market advising on how to start a business from home. There aren't quite so many books telling you how you can be a teleworker based at home – this is still a new and developing area. There are a handful of understandable books on ecommerce. This book offers you, the aspiring internet homeworker, some ideas and contacts on how you can build up a satisfying and lucrative home-based business using the fantastic facilities and resources available through the internet.

I have aimed to include sites in this book that offer genuine help to people wanting to work from home using the internet. If you have any comments on any of the sites discussed – good, bad or otherwise – I would be glad to know, since your comments may be relevant to a revised edition of the book later on. Please feel free to email me at the address shown below.

Two words of caution: there are a number of homeworking scams on the internet. While researching this book I came upon many web sites which offered 'get rich quick' schemes of one kind or another. Treat these with the utmost caution. Please also note that you are strongly advised to make your own further enquiries, and take independent qualified advice, before agreeing to part with any money or entering into any obligations, as a result of contacting web sites mentioned in this book.

All of the web sites shown in this book remain the copyright of their respective owners. The screen shots of web sites were correct at the time of going to press and may appear differently at different times. All trademarks and registered trademarks mentioned in this book are the property of their respective owners.

Finally, good hunting. A whole new world of opportunities is there for you to explore.

Laurel Alexander

laurelalexander@internet-handbooks.co.uk

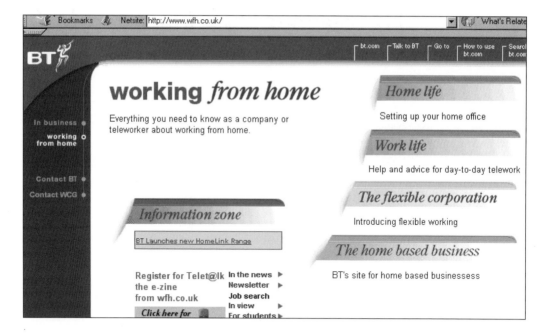

Fig. 1. (above) Homeworking with BT, a web site that tells you much of what you need to know as a company or teleworker.

Fig. 2. (below) Her Home Office has lots of advice on finding, running, operating and expanding a home business or career opportunity

1 The working from home explosion

In this chapter we will explore:

▶ *about homeworking*
▶ *the benefits of homeworking*
▶ *surviving as a homeworker*
▶ *scams and how to avoid them*
▶ *the internet explosion*
▶ *the ecommerce explosion*
▶ *freelancing*
▶ *ideas for making money through the internet and communications technology*
▶ *the Small Business Service*
▶ *funding for the small business*
▶ *teleworking*

. . . .

About homeworking

Does working from home appeal to you? If it does, that's lucky, because there is a massive demand for homeworkers of all types. Homeworkers generally come from three sectors:

1. self employed, e.g. an electrician using his home as a base or professionals like web designers who need a room for an office

2. outworkers, e.g. skilled piece workers

3. teleworkers, e.g. employees using technology installed at home by their employers to enable them to do their job from home, or those who freelance in such a capacity

But why is there such an explosion of home working? The face of work has changed enormously. Gone are the days of the large parent company, taking their workers through promotion and pay rises into retirement. Today, the average company is much smaller or if it is a large animal, then it is divided into several smaller segments. Because of increased market competition due to a rise in technology and the increase in global marketing, businesses have to cut their overheads and make speedier responses to market forces.

So where does the homeworker come in? You yourself might be one of these small businesses – working from home in order to cut your overheads. One of the ways businesses seek to cut outgoings and increase profits is to only employ people when they need them. They outsource to professionals for the duration of a project. So instead of employing someone on a permanent basis, they contract a specialised freelancer when the need arises. And more often than not the freelancer is a self-employed person based at home. Another way businesses use homeworkers is through teleworking and out-workers.

The benefits of homeworking

Lifestyle management
Looking at homeworking from the perspective of the worker, home-working offers a way to gain control of our working lives. Whereas once workers could rely on one or two jobs that lasted a lifetime, the trend now is towards constant change. The average career lasts five years. Workers need to constantly reskill and update skills to stay in work.

Your work portfolio
Today workers need to be in control of their work portfolio that could contain more than one source of income. Portfolio working is becom-ing an acceptable way to organise income and work opportunities and means we have more than one income strand. This way we can never be made completely redundant and there is always some money coming in. For example, my work portfolio contains training and development, careers guidance, writing of books and features, a reflexology practice and astrology. So I have a home-based office, but get myself out and about as well.

Security
Two key benefits of working from home are the time saved in com-muting to work and having someone permanently at home (or at least without a routine time of leaving the house), thereby increasing do-mestic security.

Family considerations
Another benefit of homeworking arises if you are a carer of adults of children. Working from home can resolve the caring problems, to a degree. However, mixing homeworking with family life can be diffi-cult. Self-discipline and effective time management are essential. Having said this, if family members are happy to help with work-related tasks, it saves on costs as you don't have to pay someone else to do them.

A financial benefit to working from home is that a proportion of costs for rooms used for work, a share of telephone and electricity bills, and part of the house running costs (e.g. council tax, etc) can be treated as business expenditure and offset against profit when calcu-lating tax. Working from home offers flexible working hours. If you work better through the night, then you can. As a homeworker you can work all hours and several days in a row, then take time off when work is slack. Work can be shifted for family commitments.

Perceptions

There can be a kudos thing attached to homeworking – or a perceived lack of it. Many people see homeworkers as not doing 'real' work and therefore as being constantly available for a chat. It is important to get across to people that your job is as important as any 'outside' work and that you cannot be disturbed. Working from home can project a poor image to some people, so it is important to have a domestic/work boundary so you ensure that clients see a professional set-up.

Motivation

On the downside, it can be hard to motivate yourself when working from home. You may find that establishing a home working routine that corresponds loosely to traditional working allows you to motivate yourself better. Another drawback to homeworking can be loneliness. Working 'outside' allows you to meet and interact with people every day. As a homeworker you may find that you hardly leave the house and only speak to people over the phone. So you need to network as much as possible. You need to get yourself out and about if you can, either as part of your work or just as 'chill-out' time.

The personal rewards

But in spite of the drawbacks, homeworking is satisfying. You work the hours you choose, you develop varied income strands, there are no travelling costs, there are no office politics to get sucked into – you don't have to make tea for anyone else, go outside to have a cigarette and you can eat a cream cake in front of the computer without it asking for a bite!

Surviving as a homeworker

To help you get the most out of working from home, here are some key tips:

1. Lay down ground rules with family and friends so that they appreciate the nature of homeworking.

2. You may need to arrange separate domestic and working space.

3. Keep up your other interests. It is harder when working from home to leave work problems behind at the end of the working day.

4. Try to establish a network of other people working from home, to combat feelings of loneliness and offer support for problems.

Health and safety for homeworkers

The use of VDUs is covered by the Health and Safety (Display Screen Equipment) Regulations 1992. When working with VDUs it is impor-

The working from home explosion ....

tant for homeworkers to adjust their workstation to a comfortable position and take breaks from work. This will help prevent undue tiredness. Remembering to stretch and change position regularly can help to reduce tiredness and prevent pains in the hands, wrists, arms, neck, shoulders or back. VDUs need to be placed in a position where lighting will not cause reflections or glare on the screen. It is also important for homeworkers to view the screen comfortably. They may need different spectacles for this; homeworkers should consult their GP or an optician if in doubt. Here is a checklist for everyone using a VDU:

1. Is the screen clear and readable, and without flicker?

2. Is the screen free from glare and reflections?

3. Are the 'brightness' and 'contrast' controls properly adjusted to prevent eyestrain?

4. Is there suitable lighting so that the fine detail on the screen can be seen and read?

5. Is the keyboard placed in the right position to allow the homeworker to work comfortably?

6. Is the screen and computer clean; is it free from dust and dirt?

7. Can the chair be adjusted to the right height so that work can be done comfortably?

8. Is the VDU placed at the right angle on the desk to allow work to be done comfortably, for example without having to make any awkward movements?

9. Is there enough space under the desk to allow free movement?

10. Is there enough space in general so that the homeworker can move freely between the work on the desk and the VDU?

Scams and how to avoid them

The Board, a subscription-only magazine that conducts investigations into scam business opportunities, states that you should be wary of the following:

(a) Companies that demand registration fees to find homework for you.

(b) Companies which offer to sell you directories of homeworking.

(c) Offers of envelope mailing, re-mailing, re-directing, or stuffing.

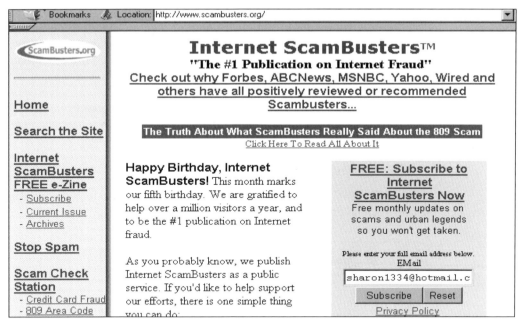

Bookmarks   Location: http://www.scambusters.org/

Internet ScamBusters™
"The #1 Publication on Internet Fraud"
Check out why Forbes, ABCNews, MSNBC, Yahoo, Wired and others have all positively reviewed or recommended Scambusters...

The Truth About What ScamBusters Really Said About the 809 Scam
Click Here To Read All About It

ScamBusters.org

Home

Search the Site

Internet
ScamBusters
FREE e-Zine
- Subscribe
- Current Issue
- Archives

Stop Spam

Scam Check
Station
- Credit Card Fraud
- 809 Area Code

Happy Birthday, Internet ScamBusters! This month marks our fifth birthday. We are gratified to help over a million visitors a year, and to be the #1 publication on Internet fraud.

As you probably know, we publish Internet ScamBusters as a public service. If you'd like to help support our efforts, there is one simple thing you can do:

FREE: Subscribe to Internet ScamBusters Now
Free monthly updates on scams and urban legends so you won't get taken.

Please enter your full email address below.
EMail
sharon1334@hotmail.c

Subscribe   Reset

Privacy Policy

Fig. 3. Scambusters is an excellent place to discover news of the latest internet scams, plus how to spot them and how to avoid them.

(d) Chain letters where you are asked to send £1 or £5 to each of five names on a list and replace one name with your own.

(e) Companies with no telephone number.

(f) Companies which are unwilling or unable to put you in touch with a couple of their satisfied customers.

The Department of Trade and Industry
The DTI has also produced a leaflet on the subject which states that such schemes as outlined above should be avoided – all of them. If you want to put a stop to junk mail, the Advertising Standards Authority suggests that you write to the offending company. If the mail continues to come through your letterbox, inform the ASA.

You can also register with the Mailing Preference Service, which aims to foster good relations between direct mail users and the general public. The MPS gives you the opportunity to have your name removed from mailing lists and claims to prevent 95 per cent of unwanted mail finding its way to you.

Trading Standards
Trading Standards bodies also advise people to be cautious about responding to advertisements which offer work from home. While many schemes are legitimate and offer real work with real wages, the following advice can help consumers avoid problems:

1. Don't send any money unless the original advertisement clearly

states how much you will be charged and exactly what it is for.

2. Don't expect to earn vast sums of money for doing very little. Make sure you know exactly how much you will earn and what you will have to do to earn it before agreeing to join a scheme.

3. If you are unsure about a particular company, contact your local Trading Standards Department to see if they have had any complaints about them.

The internet explosion

The word 'Internet' describes a collection of computers around the world that can be connected to each other via telephone lines. Here are some key scene-setting facts:

▶ *Origins* – The internet began in America in the 1960s with four computers owned by the Department of Defence. The reason it was set up was to swap information between agency sites in the event of a nuclear bomb falling on one of the computers.

▶ *Universities* – In the early 1980s, computer users within universities were beginning to get the idea of connecting their machines for information exchange. BITNET (Because It's Time Network) connected IBM mainframes around the educational community and mail services began. BITNET was set up as the first academic network that linked Yale University and the City University of New York. Listserv software was developed for this network and later others. Gateways were developed to connect BITNET with the internet and allowed exchange of email and discussion lists.

▶ *Science* – The American government wanting to invest in this new technology established funding for the National Science Foundation's own network called NSFNet in the late 1980s. This was a nationwide educational network linking academic research establishments and universities.

▶ *British universities* – then joined in by establishing JANET (the Joint Academic Network). This linked academics throughout the UK.

▶ *National networks* – quickly developed into international ones through gateways that have been developed by commercial organisations employed by the American National Science Foundation. Gateways are specific systems enabling people on one network to access information on another network. It was from this point that the internet as we know it today evolved.

▶ *The world wide web* – Another milestone in the birth of the internet was passed at the European Laboratory for Particle Physics in Switzerland in 1989. Here was developed the concept of the 'world wide web'. This was based on hypertext links which give any computer linked to the web access to information published on any other computer linked to the web.

▶ *The Netscape web browser* – Around this time web browsers were also created. Marc Andreessen at the National Centre for Supercomputing Applications moved to become the brains behind Netscape Corporation, which produced the first really successful graphical browser. It later faced competition from Microsoft which developed its own highly popular web browser, Internet Explorer, which a majority of people now use.

▶ *The commercial internet* – 1990 saw the first commercial company to provide access to the internet. Delphi was the first national commercial online service to offer internet access to subscribers in 1992.

▶ *The information superhighway* – The 1990s saw the information superhighway really taking off. The term appears to have been first used by American Vice President Al Gore.

It's difficult to estimate how many people are online throughout the world, but according to a survey compiled by Nua Internet Surveys as of February 2000 (email: surveys@nua.ie), the world total is somewhere around 275 million.

Accessing the internet
In order to get onto the internet, or to build your own web site, you need: a computer, a modem, a telephone line and an account with an internet access provider Once you're connected, you can surf all the web sites you like. Then you could go onto the next stage: planning, building and publishing your own web site.

What does having your own web site mean?
A web site can include pictures and text to promote your products and services. It can be viewed by anyone on the world wide web: millions of people in over 110 countries, 24 hours per day, 365 days per year. You can have a web site purely for information or you can use it to sell a product or service. This is called electronic commerce – ecommerce for short.

The ecommerce explosion

The number of people with internet access is currently growing at the phenomenal rate of 10% every month, with the value of financial transactions on the internet doubling every three months. So how

The working from home explosion ....

do you sort the basics of starting an ecommerce business?

Your product
First you need something to sell. If you feel you have a great product or service that you could sell to an internet consumer in a wide geographical market, then you ought to be selling it online.

Your retail pitch
You need to own or rent some web space where your shop web site will live. Web space is a virtual plot of land where your shop web site will be built and seen by visitors. Find out whether or not you can operate a commercial web site from any web space you might get free with your internet service provider; not all allow freespace to be used for commercial purposes.

Internet retailing software
Then you need some shop-building software. To build a shop web site you will have to use special software such as Dreamteam Design's EROL (Electronic Retail Online). The most common way of taking payment is to obtain permission from your bank to operate a 'merchant account' by which you can take credit card payments. Internet security technology has improved to such a degree that this is possibly the safest way of transferring credit card details.

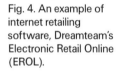

Fig. 4. An example of internet retailing software, Dreamteam's Electronic Retail Online (EROL).

A good shop-building package will automatically create the correct secure environment for receiving and sending credit card numbers. You can receive orders via email (a good shop building soft-

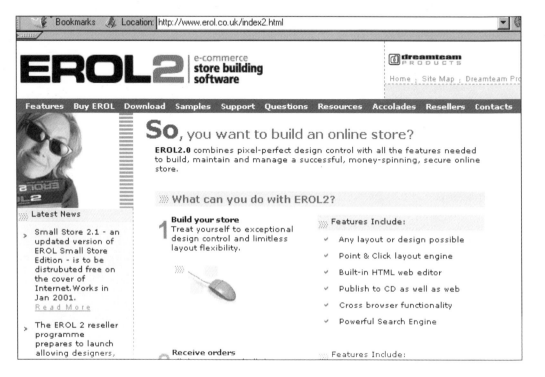

ware will provide you with the facilities to do this securely). You can then accept the order and sort out the payment using more traditional means such as getting back to the customer by phone or by ordinary mail. Speak to your bank about the opportunities and facilities it provides for internet business.

▶ *Forecast* – Revenue from ecommerce by 2002 is estimated to become almost £5 billions.

Profile of an internet consumer
1. The male/female split is around 70% and 30% for all internet users (women are however emerging as a growing market force on the internet).

2. More young people between 22 and 30 use the internet.

3. High income groups are heavily represented as using the internet.

4. 70% of internet users shop regularly on the internet.

5. Internet consumers are well educated, with a large proportion of them educated at university level.

6. Most users have a background in the professions, management, finance and education.

7. The two main reasons that internet users give for using the net are information and entertainment. So, information and entertainment add value to a web site.

▶ *Britain* – UK ecommerce transactions during 1999 were expected to be worth around £2.8bn with the potential to grow tenfold over the next three years (IDC Research Report).

▶ *New industries* – Ecommerce will create jobs in new industries such as 'information brokering' and old industries such as distribution and logistics.

Freelancing

Freelancing from home means you have a home-based office. You may either run your business entirely from home or via a mixture of inside and outside work. As a freelancer you are self-employed and are responsible for marketing your business, delivering your business, financial management and business planning. You could choose to be a portfolio freelance and have several areas of expertise to offer. The more you can offer, the more money you can make – the less likely you are to be out of work.

The working from home explosion ....

Ideas for making money through the internet

Authoring web pages	Online auctions
Bilingual word processing	Recruitment agency
Book selling	Research
Bookkeeping and accountancy	Selling and supporting
Brokering services	computer hardware
Customised products	Selling collectibles
CV production	Selling of music CDs
Data conversion	Selling of other people's
Dating agency	products
Designing & setting up	Setting up and selling of
databases	emailing lists
Desktop publishing	Shareware internet service
E-commerce consultancy	provider
Financial services	Souvenir sales
Graphic design	Tourism
Information brokering	Training services
Law	Translation
Mailshots	Web authoring
Manuscript preparation	Writing
Office supplies	Writing and selling software

The Small Business Service

The UK government recently announced proposals for a new Small Business Service with effect from April 2001. It is modelled partly on the Small Business Administration in the USA. The following is taken from Working Brief published by the Unemployment Unit & Youthaid Research, Information, Campaigning. Its address is: 322 St John Street, London EC1V 4NU.

'A new Small Business Service was also announced. This will have a strong remit to deliver the advice and support that firms need to grow and bring together different parts of the DTI, Better Regulation Unit and the DfEE from April 2001. Modelled partly on the Small Business Administration in the USA, the new service will provide small business with:

1. Options to cut compliance burden.

2. Automated payroll service for small employers.

3. Expansion of quarterly employers PAYE scheme from a limit of £600 a month to £1,000 a month.

4. New Inland Revenue business support teams to discuss problems with any business within 48 hours.

Fig. 5. The web site of the new Small Business Service, recently set up by the UK Department of Trade and Industry.

5. New business advice service from Customs and Excise for exporters and importers.

6. New Enterprise Support Initiative, including a dedicated helpline for new employers.

7. Discounts for internet-filed electronic tax returns.

There will also be measures to encourage investment. The Government will extend 40% first year capital allowances for another year; together with proposals for R&D tax credits for small and medium-sized companies.'

Funding for the small business

Grants and funding for the new or very small business are limited and depend very much on the geographical area in which you run your business.

(a) If you are unemployed you could qualify for a grant of up to £1,380 towards set-up costs.

(b) Some areas operate the New Entrepreneurs Challenge Fund, which provides a grant of £1,000, loans, on-going business support and training.

The working from home explosion ....

(c) You may qualify for a grant to meet 50% of the costs toward Diagnostic and Consultancy support – this could be useful if you plan to develop your business. You will probably have to show 12 months' trading accounts to qualify.

(d) Discretionary grants may be available under Regional Selective Assistance if you live in or are relocating to an Assisted Area, are creating employment or safeguarding existing jobs. This includes your own job.

(e) If you live in, or are located in the East and West Midlands, you may also qualify for a Regional Enterprise Grant.

(f) If you live in a rural area you may be eligible for a grant towards the conversion costs of redundant buildings. In 1995/96, almost £12m was contributed to workspace programmes.

Ask your local Business Links for information about what you may be eligible. Phone: 0345-567 765

Being a freelancer is hard work. You are all departments of a business rolled into one. However, you cannot be made redundant – and you'll never be bored!

Teleworking

'According to the Labour Force Survey, teleworking is growing at the rate of 15 per cent a year, and about five per cent of the working population is using Internet communications. By 2004, this figure will have reached 10 per cent. Clearly, this goes hand in hand with the growth of SOHOs in the Internet industry.' (Alan Denby, TCA director).

Teleworking or telecommuting is the art of working from home using technology, either for an employer or for yourself.

1. To engage in teleworking there are start-up costs involved, the most expensive being the cost of the computer itself as well as a modem and a printer.

2. A rewritable CD-ROM is also a good idea. With this, a large volume of work can then be saved to one disk ready to be sent back to an employer or client.

3. A scanner will further the scope of work you can take on as pictures are usually used for any desktop publishing. Scanners can also be used for inputting a text document into a word processing package for changes to be made.

4. Minor costs involve floppy disks, printing paper, inks or toner car-

tridges for printers. An allowance should be made for extra electricity used and slightly higher telephone bills as most of your communications will be made via the telephone. Of course if you work for an employer, they will provide all this equipment – if you work for yourself, the buck stops with you.

Solitary teleworking
This kind of working structure, in which an individual works at a location that is separate from the central office, can take one of two forms – fixed or mobile. With fixed location solitary teleworking, the individual works from a single location – probably at home. With mobile solitary teleworking, the individual will travel between different locations, using mobile and other kinds of communication systems to communicate with the central office.

Group teleworking
With group-based teleworking, people work remotely from the centre. The group may comprise any number of individuals and involve group-based working and social activities. This kind of teleworking can be further divided into two kinds:

1. Tele-centre and satellite offices that are used by employees who are employed specifically to work at a distance but who have not previously experienced working within the central organisation. Freelance and consultants often operate within such structures.

2. Tele-cottages – offices that are equipped with the relevant communications infrastructures but are used by a variety of different people who work for different organisations, often on a freelance basis.

Flexible teleworking
Flexible teleworking can be considered to be a mixture of solitary and group teleworking. Groups form, sometimes in a 'virtual' fashion, to undertake specific tasks; communications and groups are carried out in flexible ways, in various locations, at different times and using a variety of technological aids.

New small internet businesses
Attracted by a flexible working lifestyle and lucrative project rates, an increasing number of people with new media skills are choosing to set up their own small internet businesses. For clients looking to buy new media services, outsourcing to small businesses or freelancers means they can avoid the fixed costs associated with maintaining employees in-house, or paying the high fees charged by full-service agencies. According to the TCA (Telework, Telecottage and Telecentre Association), more than 1.3 million people in the UK telework are using electronic communications, without going to a formal workplace.

The working from home explosion ....

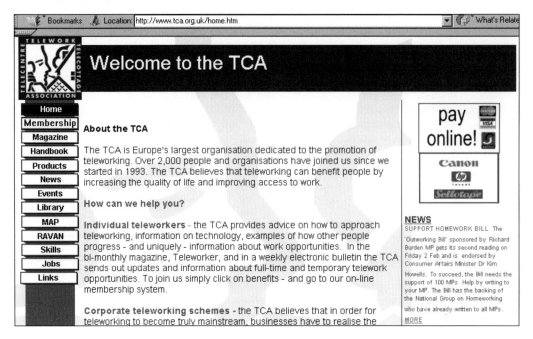

Based on the UK Labour Force Survey of Spring 1997, the Teleworker Magazine reported that the current number of teleworkers in Great Britain is 987,000, which is 4% of total employment. One third of employed teleworkers are in banking, finance and insurance.

More Internet Handbooks to help you

Where to Find it on the Internet, Kye Valongo (second edition).

2 Homeworking business ideas

In this chapter we will explore:

▶ *desktop publishing*
▶ *general home business ideas*
▶ *law*
▶ *the training business*
▶ *the travel business*
▶ *web-based opportunities*
▶ *web design and authoring*
▶ *writing and illustration*

. . . .

How this chapter can help you

This chapter describes web sites which can help you:

1. Use some hints on running your DTP business.

2. Access a range of home-based business ideas, articles, awards, a bookstore, business opportunities and chat.

3. Design your web site, and get into ezine publishing.

4. Own the complete reprint rights to a range of business reports, books and guides including full reseller rights.

5. Find out how to design online training courses.

6. Explore services that allow you to operate a home-based travel agency.

7. Look at tools for web authoring.

8. Get some ideas of web design pricing.

9. Visit a digital marketplace for online content creators, online writers, editors and publishers.

10. Visit web sites set up to help copy editors, proofreading and editorial freelancers.

11. Access assignments for newspaper and magazine journalists, designers and artists throughout the UK.

12. Explore electronic book publishing.

13. Visit a professional association representing technical authors, illustrators, and other specialists in the field of scientific and technical communication.

14. Purchase books on advertising, copywriting and marketing subjects and manuals for ad-industry freelances, creative professionals and marketing personnel.

15. Purchase a career guide for freelancing for technical service agencies and independent contracting and consulting.

16. Get onto a free internet directory of independent writers & artists.

17. Make your knowledge pay through writing and publishing your own ebook.

Desktop publishing

Desktop Publishing
http://desktoppub.about.com/compute/desktoppub/
msubprice.htm
Visit this site to get some idea of pricing your DTP business. It also contains information on other business aspects of DTP including freelancing and relevant software. You can also take part in a chat room and receive a site newsletter. There is a useful list of related sites dealing with topics such as technical writing and publishing.

The Hit Squad Freelancers
http://www.hitsquad.co.uk/free.htm
This site is intended for freelance DTP professionals or 'Hitsquadders'. So whether you are a PC or Mac user, a visit to this site might bring in some work. Click onto the links for Freelance or Vacancy to explore current opportunities.

General home business ideas

Home-Based Business Ideas
http://kwilliams.bizhosting.com/idea1.html
Through the home page of this site you can access home-based business ideas, articles, awards, a bookstore, business opportunities and chat. You can advertise your business, design your homepage and get into ezine publishing.

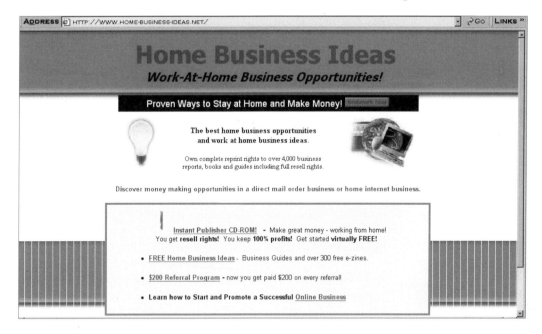

Home Business Ideas
http://www.home-business-ideas.net/
Some of the best home business opportunities and work-at-home business ideas could be found on this site. For example, you could acquire the complete reprint and reseller rights to more than 4,000 business reports, books and guides. Explore some moneymaking opportunities in a direct mail order business or home internet business.

Fig. 6. At the web site of Home Business Ideas you can discover how to make money with a direct mail order or home internet business.

Law

The Freelance Solicitors Group
http://members.aol.com/pjmiller00/freelance.html
The Freelance Solicitors Group represents the interests of those solicitors in England and Wales who work as solicitors for others on a locum, contract or freelance basis. Its activities include: a network of professional and social contacts, advice to members, making the Law Society aware of the interests of freelance solicitors, and providing a list of prospective employers and entries in *The Law Society's Directory* of those members available for freelance, contract or locum work.

The training business

Campus America 'The Learning Manager'
http://www.campus.com/
Campus America has 20-year track record in information technology for education. It offers tools for curriculum development, instructional design, and course delivery. You could use it in traditional training or virtual learning environments using PC and client/server for distance learning, interactive multimedia, computer managed learning, computer aided instruction, competency based training, open learning, flexible delivery and knowledge production.

Centra Software: Symposium
http://www.cena.com
Centra provides some state-of-the-art education and training programs. These are designed to help presenters, educators, curriculum developers, content developers, instructional designers, tutors, systems administrators, and other business professionals in their use of its educational package, Symposium. It offers Symposium-delivered sessions, tutor-led classroom training, education consulting, content developer program, and certification programs. Its courses include modules on designing sessions, creating content, converting existing content, using Symposium Course Builder, best practices for presenters and leaders, holding effective Symposium meetings, and other topics.

Cinecom Corporation
http://www.cinecom.com/
Would you like to explore the potential for video conferencing and internet/intranet connectivity? Cinecom supplies multimedia delivery systems for virtual classroom environments, software for virtual education, and corporate training. It offers user applications for virtual education (distance learning), a virtual help desk, online tutoring, corporate training, virtual meetings or conferences. Its product – Virtual Educator – offers more than video-conferencing: it delivers a complete distance learning solution for use over local or wider area networks, and the internet. You can use Virtual Educator as a tutor-controlled learning environment with web-based classes, multipoint video and audio, tutor-led web discussions, shared whiteboard and more.

Class Net
http://classnet.cc.iastate.edu/
ClassNet is world wide web server software that can help you to manage internet class activities. Using this service you can create classes, design assignments, administer and grade your students, and conduct online communication between learners and tutors.

Darryl Sink

http://www.dsink.com/

From the home page, you can link into a range of instructional design products. Based on the principles of instructional design theory, Darryl Sink has developed learning tools that both supplement its range of workshops, and function as standalone products. Its main course development software is called CourseWriter 2.0.

E-CourseWare

http://www.e-course.com/products.htm

E-Course is a new series of software products that provide a quick, hands-on introduction to fundamental application skills. It makes use of on-screen tutorials that run over the live application, along with an exercise-filled work text.

Flax

http://www.cms.dmu.ac.uk/coursebook/flax/

Flax helps you create interactive web pages and to collate materials you have created along with other resources on the web. From the home page you can see examples, view sample coursebooks, download material, and get onto a mailing list.

Fig. 7. FLAX lets you develop interactive courses on the web.

In Depth Learning Web

http://www.indepthl.com/

In Depth provides online tools for learning, online learning systems and CBT, authorware, director, and macromedia consulting, computer workshops for teachers, 3D illustration, web publishing, databases, and programming. IDL bases its curricula designs on the

29

models of Gardner, Schank, and Kovalick, particularly goal-based scenarios and integrated thematic instruction models. It also develops ISD-based solutions for training problems. The curriculum is delivered on the web, on CD-ROM, or through traditional print media.

Lecture Web
http://lectureweb.turnaround.com.au/
Lecture Web offers a solution to publishing documents for a distributed online teaching environment.

Lotus Learning Space
http://www.lotus.com/
You can access some powerful training software through this site. It has some strong collaborative features, plus messaging tools and a course administration system.

Quest
http://www.allencomm.com/
This site provides tools and services that focus on the whole process of successful multimedia development: pre-authoring, instructional design, multimedia authoring, training delivery, management, custom courseware solutions, and consulting. Other links will take you to solutions including events, the Academy of Multimedia and custom courseware development. There is a download option as well as a search facility and contact button.

QuestWriter
http://www.peak.org/qw
This is a site developed at Oregon State University. It offers a set of tools to support online course materials that you can use to supplement your own course materials as well as for running completely online classes.

Question Mark
http://www.qmark.com/
Since being set up ten years ago, Question Mark has established itself as a leader in computerised assessment software. It creates software that is both easy to use and very secure, making it a good fit for almost any type of training organisation or business. Question Mark software is used by organisations in more than fifty countries. Major corporations, universities, schools, and governments use it to administer a wide range of tests and surveys. Among its products is QML, a new platform-independent method of maintaining question databases for surveys and assessments.

Technical Writing
http://techwriting.miningco.com/arts/techwriting/
Explore the links relating to editing, classes, newsgroups, organisa-

tions and publishing. The site includes articles about successful inter-viewing and freelancing.

WebCT
http://homebrew.cs.ubc.ca/webct/
This well-regarded site developed at the University of British Colum-bia gives you access to a highly effective and well designed tool for creating your own courseware on the internet. WebCT offers an at-tractive and easy-to-use environment for creating sophisticated web-based courses that would otherwise beyond the ability of the non-computer programmer. It makes extensive use of readymade tem-plates.

WebMentor
http://www.avilar.com
This site sells a software product designed for web-based education and distance learning. There are five buttons on the home page, which take you into the nitty-gritty of the site. From there you can find out about authoring, the product, demo courses, support, colla-boration, the management team, pricing, contact points, and press releases.

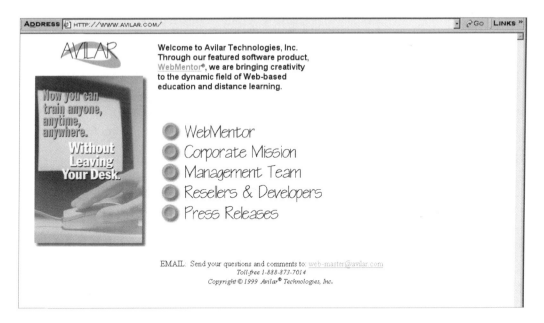

zXcv
http://www.zxcv.com/
This site can help you with tools and expertise to meet the organisa-tional development needs associated with distance learning through a suite of web-conferencing and chat tools.

Fig. 8. WebMentor can help you develop a creative online training programme.

The travel business

ATA Travel Agency Sellers
http://www.cbimembers.com/index1.htm
This site sells travel agency programmes that will allow you to operate your own licensed home-based travel agency over the internet. You can read through its online brochure, read about the program in detail, and download a demo version travel agency.

Quantum Travel
http://www.jr-corp.com/quantum/
If you are looking for a home-based opportunity in the travel industry visit this site.

Web-based home-working opportunities

Locate Me
http://www.locateme.co.uk/
Locate-Me is all about helping small businesses to present their services and product on the internet and then helping customers to locate those businesses on the web. You are invited to complete an online registration form to apply for a start-up kit. This includes a training manual, a pack of order forms, a pack of claim forms, a pack of leaflets, a price list and a channel sales earning list.

SyberShopper
http://www.sybershopper.com/
With SyberShopper you no longer need to shop around for the cheapest goods. Just enter your requirements into the site, or telephone them through and at least ten companies will compete for your custom offering you their best deal – cars, holidays, insurance, gas, telephone, electrical goods, CDs, videos, books and more. As a distributor for SyberShopper you receive your own company web site. You then have three ways of earning income – recruiting distributors, finding companies to compete for these orders, and encouraging other people to use the service.

Skybiz
http://skybusiness.com/lat2000
http://www.skynary.com/nowmeb
Skybiz says it is the ideal business with huge income potential and no paperwork. You are invited to buy your own 15-megabyte web site with unlimited pages for approximately £65 with tools to design it for your business or family use.

Essentials Direct
http://www.essentialsdirect.com/001527
First, you can buy all your known brand groceries and other products at supermarket prices or less, delivered to your door. Second, you can

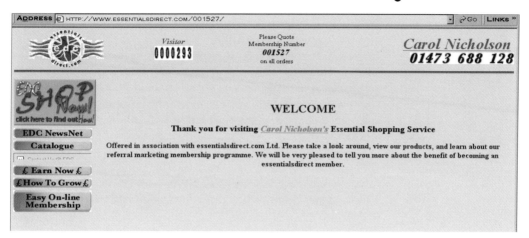

Fig. 9. Essential Direct. Find out about a referral marketing membership programme.

earn money from others doing the same. The companies involved include a well-known cash and carry company as well as many other household names.

Future World
http://future-world.com/cgi-bin/catalog/31215
This company offers you an opportunity to make money from every time zone on earth, even while you sleep. Its products include books, tapes, CD-ROMs and multimedia software. The subjects cover health, languages, memory, personal development, travel, music, directories, business and much more. If you join, they say you'll enjoy operating from your home office with no stock, equipment, employees or rent, earn commission on product sales and distributors' bonuses, no need to do paperwork, take calls, fill orders or ship – head office does it all and no need for your own credit card merchant status or worry about verifying personal cheques.

Web design and authoring

Association for Learning Technology
http://www.warwick.ac.uk/alt-E/rolling/resource/84
Web-O-Matic and Java tools for web authoring are available through this University of Warwick site.

Bjis Web Authoring
http://www.bjis.demon.co.uk/
This practical and user-friendly site offers help for web authors wanting to learn page creation and site design. You can also access information about tools and tutorials and links to other useful sites. The author, Ian Scott, works as an Information Officer for a large UK college. Before that he spent a couple of years doing desk top publishing, web authoring and database development for a small business.

Homeworking business ideas ....

Tactile
http://www.tactile.co.uk/us.htm
Tactile was formed in 1997 to explore the creative possibilities of the internet. For each web-building project it pulls in a team of associate companies and freelancers to complement in-house skills including copywriters, designers, flash programmers, sound consultants and video consultants. The site showcases some of the work it has done for clients.

Web Design
http://webdesign.tqn.com/compute/webdesign/msubpricing.htm
This is a page about web design pricing with related links and information.

Web Monkey – Teaching Tool
http://www.hotwired.com/webmonkey/teachingtool/
Web Monkey is a very popular and essential site for anyone who wants to find out more about web development. From the home page you can learn step-by-step about authoring, design, multimedia, e-business, programming and backend (all with sub topics). There is a button for jobs and contacts and you can sign up for *Elbow Grease*, a daily newsletter.

Writing and illustration

Book Idea
http://www.bookidea.com/map/map.html
Book Idea is an online magazine for small publishers, self-publishers, authors, and freelance writing professionals. Each edition is packed with expert information, resources, interactive areas and support designed to help you build a better business and make more money. New articles, information and features are added all the time. Book Idea is published by Bookhome Publishing, which produces books and reports about the writing and publishing business, and about small business generally.

Content Exchange
http://www.content-exchange.com/
This is a digital marketplace for online content creators, writers, editors and publishers to advertise their services. You can create a free profile in its talent database. This feature can be accessed from the main navigation bar. You can search its database of paying online venues, and in its Classified Ad area you can place an ad describing the type of work you seek – existing content that you are offering for sale and so on. There is a charge for placing ads. In addition to operating its Content Exchange service, the company operates an email discussion list.

Copy Editors
http://www.tamu-commerce.edu/coas/journalism/resources/
315copyedit.html
This is rather a long web site address, but copy editors will find lots of useful links on this handy page.

Dot Journalism
http://www.journalism.co.uk/
Jobs for newspaper and magazine journalists, designers and artists throughout the UK including freelancers can be found here.

eBookNews.com
http://www.ebooknews.com
This site provides recent news about developing electronic book technology for consumers and authors, as well as ebook sales and electronic book publishing. You can also access ebook reviews and downloadable ebooks.

Editorial Freelancers' Home Page
http://www.nerc.com/-freelancer/welcome.html
On this site you will find professional resources, information, and help for editors, proofreaders, writers, desktop and electronic publishers, and web page designers.

Edward Twentyman Resources
http://www.etr.co.uk/
This site would seem to represent the only British agency to specialise exclusively in bringing publishers and freelancers together.

Fig. 10. Edward Twentyman Resources invites you to fill in a questionnaire and hopefully get offered some freelance work.

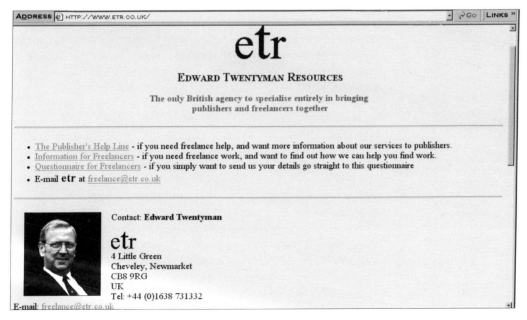

Homeworking business ideas ....

Freelancers.co.uk
http://www.freelancers.co.uk/
Link into freelance editing and proofreading courses. Information on
on-screen editing is also available.

FreelanceSearch
http://www.freelancesearch.com/
FreelanceSearch.com was developed to fill the need for an efficient
portal site for freelance writers, editors, and translators. It presents the
contact and experience information of its freelancers in a simple and
easily navigable directory. It offers a forum through which freelance
writers, editors, proofreaders, and translators can advertise their individual skills at a web site that has been successfully promoted under
the terms that potential employers are using to locate these types of
services. Each listing contains the contact information of the freelancer as well as information regarding his or her previous work
experience and other optional information.

Freelance Writers
http://freelancewrite.about.com/arts/freelancewrite/mbody.htm
You'll find plenty of links, ideas for different types of writing, a free
newsletter, articles and software for the writer on this site.

Institute of Scientific and Technical Communicators
http://www.write-on.co.uk/istc.htm
The ISTC is a professional association, based in the UK, representing
technical authors, illustrators, and other specialists in the field of
scientific and technical communication. The ISTC Independent
Authors' Special Interest Group has been formed by freelance members of the ISTC, with the following aims: sharing job and contract
information; sharing business skills; sharing technical knowledge and
provision of opportunities for informal contact. Membership is open
to all members of the ISTC who are freelancers or have an interest in
freelance work.

Internet Handbooks
http://www.internet-handbooks.co.uk/
There are opportunities for suitably qualified and experienced authors
to write or contribute to Internet Handbooks.

Know-How Publications
http://www.know-how.org.uk/
Know-How publications are publishers of electronic books on advertising, copywriting and marketing subjects and manuals for ad-
industry freelances, creative professionals and marketing personnel.
They will shortly be adding a new and exciting list of titles of more
general interest to independent businesspersons.

Fig. 11. The home page of Internet Handbooks, the publishers of this book. It contains lots of free help on using the internet.

Making Money in Technical Writing
http://www.wordesign.com/BookReviewPeterKent.htm
Peter Kent's 270-page career guide is published by Macmillan General Reference, and covers freelancing for technical service agencies and independent contracting and consulting.

Published.com
http://www.published.com/
The site offers a free internet directory of independent writers and artists. It is designed to help promote the creative work of independent writers, musicians, illustrators, ezine publishers, filmmakers, and other independent artists. You can add listings of your own creative work for free.

Society of Freelance Editors and Proofreaders
http://www.sfep.demon.co.uk
This is the main UK membership organisation for publishing industry freelancers. Its web site has a corporate members' page that lists publishing firms that use freelancers and the rates of pay they offer.

Freelance Journal
http://home.eunet.no/~trondhu/
Freelance Writers.net is a web site for writers, editors, publishers, poets and readers and anyone interested in publishing, editing and writing. There are areas for poetry, fiction, literary works and columns about writing by writers.

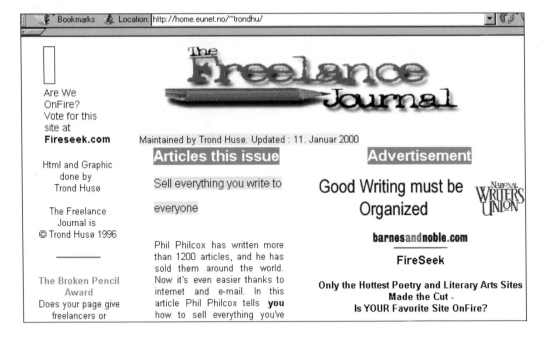

10money.com
http://www.10money.com/myks.htm
Make your knowledge sell through writing and publishing your own ebook.

More Internet Handbooks to help you

1001 Web Sites for Writers, Nick Daws.
Building a Web Site on the Internet, Brendan Murphy.
Creating a Home Page on the Internet, Richard Cochrane.
Running a Shop on the Internet, Graham Jones.
The Internet for Writers, Nick Daws.

3 Looking for freelance work

In this chapter we will explore:

▶ *freelance opportunities*
▶ *associations for freelancers*

. . . .

How this chapter can help you

This chapter describes web sites which can help you:

1. See the site that offers to match freelancers with businesses intent on outsourcing projects that can be completed remotely.

2. Get yourself onto databases and directories of consultants, freelancers and contractors.

3. Register to access IT job contracts, news, information on recruiters and training, and advice for new contractors.

4. Network with other freelancers.

5. Search for freelance work in the daily nationals.

6. Someone wants a freelancer – put in a bid and you might get the work!

Freelance opportunities

Ants.com
http://www.ants.com/ants/
Ants offers to match freelancers with businesses who want to outsource projects that can be completed remotely. They say: 'Find and bid on projects that match your schedule and skills. With over 70,000 members and more than 70 categories of job descriptions, Ants.com is the fastest growing marketplace for freelance work, expanding at a rate of about one percent per day. Headquartered in Santa Barbara, California, Ants.com is dedicated to creating a liquid marketplace for the trillion-dollar worldwide freelance services market. Companies looking to outsource projects – from programming to translation to marketing to design – can quickly meet their needs at Ants.com, drawing from the largest pool of qualified freelancers and independent workers in the world. Ants.com is a privately held company backed by Bertelsmann Ventures'. The main project categories are administrative, design, computer, financial, legal, marketing, translation, writing, and other.

Consult Direct
http://www.kelwin.co.uk/ConsultDirect/bout.HTM
Here you can find an unaffiliated directory of consultants, freelancers and contractors. Advertisers can present themselves with a company profile, a CV or a resume.

Looking for freelance work...

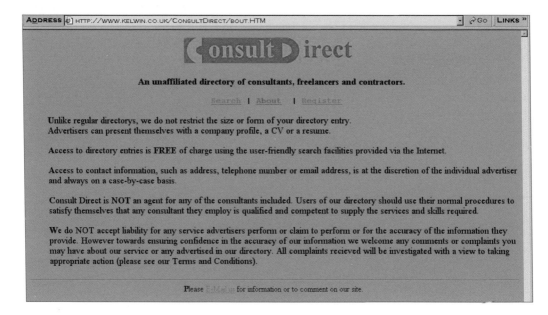

ADDRESS ⬝ HTTP://WWW.KELWIN.CO.UK/CONSULTDIRECT/BOUT.HTM ⬝ Go ⬝ LINKS »

⟨onsult ⟩irect

An unaffiliated directory of consultants, freelancers and contractors.

Search | About | Register

Unlike regular directorys, we do not restrict the size or form of your directory entry.
Advertisers can present themselves with a company profile, a CV or a resume.

Access to directory entries is **FREE** of charge using the user-friendly search facilities provided via the Internet.

Access to contact information, such as address, telephone number or email address, is at the discretion of the individual advertiser and always on a case-by-case basis.

Consult Direct is NOT an agent for any of the consultants included. Users of our directory should use their normal procedures to satisfy themselves that any consultant they employ is qualified and competent to supply the services and skills required.

We do NOT accept liability for any service advertisers perform or claim to perform or for the accuracy of the information they provide. However towards ensuring confidence in the accuracy of our information we welcome any comments or complaints you may have about our service or any advertised in our directory. All complaints recieved will be investigated with a view to taking appropriate action (please see our Terms and Conditions).

Please E-Mail us for information or to comment on our site.

Fig. 12. Consult Direct is another directory for freelancers to get onto. Use it to showcase your expertise online.

eLance.com
http://www.elance.com

This lively site helps buyers and sellers of freelance jobs locate one another, and work out the terms of business. The site can be used as a platform for communication and delivery of service. Jobs are either open for bidding or posted at a fixed price. The service is mostly oriented toward high-tech projects, but administrative and research opportunities are also on offer. They say: 'From web design, logos and writing to software programming, business research and much more, eLance provides the platform to connect, communicate, and complete your projects. Buyers can post a project description and receive bids from service providers, or buy directly from thousands of service listings. eLance support features include the Work Space for file sharing and remote delivery, service provider certifications, feedback ratings, and an international billing and payment system Since September 1999, more than 160,000 individuals and businesses from 140 countries have registered on eLance to get their projects done.' September 2000 saw the announcement of $50 million new funding into the service.

eWanted.com
http://www.ewanted.com/services/

This is another established way to market your services to a potentially huge market. Just post your details in the Freelance Work section, seen by thousands of potential buyers every day. You could reach a whole new sector of your market. In October 1998, the company launched its first dynamic marketplace site – where buyers post what they want, and sellers find instant customers. Today, it hosts tens of thousands of buyer requests – more than 1,000 categories of wanted items and services – including freelance services of all kinds. The service features an anonymous email system that protects the privacy of user accounts

Freelance BBS
http://www.freelancebbs.com/
The Freelance Bulletin Board Service helps freelancers and their prospective employers to find each other. Using a simple online form, you can either search for a project or a talented individual in several professions. They say: 'Feel free to post projects and availabilities. For more precise results, you can try using two advanced search forms: one for available projects and another one for freelancers in search of work.' After you post your ad (whether it's a resume or a job availability), you can still make changes to it or delete it if necessary. To do that, find your ad through the search form, go to 'details' and look for the Modify and Delete buttons at the bottom of the ad. You will be asked for the password which you chose when posting your ad.

Freelance.com
http://www.freelance.com
Freelance.com is a new online professional services marketplace that connects pre-screened freelance professionals around the world with Fortune 1000 and market-leading companies that need them every day. It says it is the only global online professional services network offering companies a dedicated Account Manager to ensure excellent matches and long-term support. It aims to meet the exploding needs of multinational and regional companies nearly anywhere. Originally established in France in 1996, the Freelance.com organisation is now headquartered in New York, and has offices in 14 countries worldwide.

Freelance Professionals
Home Page
About Us
Join Our Community
Project Mailing List
Services
Companies
About Us
Media Relations
Reach a Representative
Home Page

Freelance Informer
http://www.freelanceinformer.co.uk
Resources for the IT contracting sector can be found through this home page. Register to access job postings, news, information on recruiters and training, and advice for new contractors. There are links to directory, finance, first timers, IR35, jobs, legal, news, overseas, skills and a yearbook. 'There are 3,299 jobs today at Freelance Informer.' The service is a division of Reed Business Information.

Freelance Jobs
http://www.freelance-jobs.net/
Freelance Jobs describes itself as a major source of jobs, career advancement opportunities, and employment information for the freelance industry.

Looking for freelance work...

Freelancers.net
http://www.freelancers.net/
Freelancers.net maintains an open database of UK and global internet freelancers. It costs nothing to get yourself listed and it is free to search for freelancers: 'Matching freelance and contract internet and multimedia professionals to freelance and contract opportunities.' The Freelancers Network gives you your own easy-to-remember web address which you can point to your own portfolio, CV, or resume.

Freelance Online
http://www.freelanceonline.com/
The operators of the site say that they intend to make it a primary resource centre for small business owners and the self-employed. You can access jobs, message boards, a searchable directory of over 700 freelancers, frequently asked questions, resources, and net-working opportunities for freelance professionals. Run from Philadelphia, USA, the site serves freelancers and employers already established in the web community and those who are new to the web. The fee for full membership is $15 per year. This includes a listing in the directory and access to the jobs page. Freelancers can post their profiles with FOL and can even obtain links to their own home pages (a reciprocal link is appreciated but not mandatory). 'Browse through our directory and find the group or groups that best fit your skills, then register your information with us.' In the Open Forum you can discuss issues with other freelancers. The resource area lists helpful links and information on various aspects of freelancing. The service was launched in 1996.

Freelance Marketplace
http://247malls.com/OS/cj/ants.htm
This is where you can find your marketplace community for indepen-dent contractors and freelance opportunities. They say: 'Welcome to your freelance marketplace, your marketplace community for inde-pendent contractors and businesses. Browse through the job listing to find freelance opportunities that match your interests including writing, marketing, translation, programming and design.'

Freelance Work Exchange
http://www.freelanceworkexchange.com/
The site offers a free report describing 50 top-producing freelance markets, together with a freelance directory and project directory.

FreetimeJobs.com
http://www.freejob.com/
This site seeks to match ordinary people of all skill levels with small businesses that need help. From a few hours of seasonal work to longer term projects, there are lots of opportunities to explore.

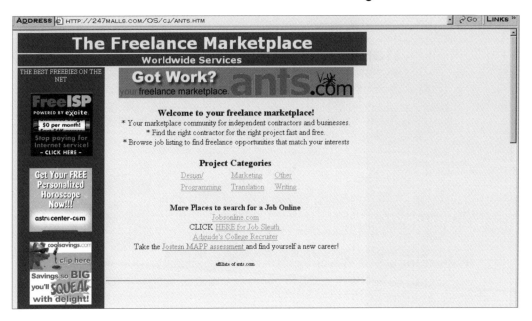

Fig. 13. The Freelance Marketplace. Want a freelance job to match your interest? The answer could be here.

Guru
http://www.guru.com/
Founded in April 1999, Guru.com describes itself as the web's premier exchange for connecting independent professionals with contract projects. With more than 300,000 independent professionals and over 30,000 hiring clients registered as of late 2000, Guru has been recognized as a top-ranking resource by *PC Magazine*, Yahoo!, *Internet Life*, *Forbes* and other industry leaders. Based in San Francisco, it has raised $63 million from investors to develop its services. They say: 'Our convenient online system makes it easy to log billable hours, manage your expenses, and generate invoices. Our street-smart articles and advice columns help you tackle the challenges of guru life.' Registration is free.

HireAbility
http://www.hireability.com/
This is a service company that provides a link between businesses needing specialised work performed and those with the ability to get the job done. It offers freelancing, telecommuting, contract, consulting, writing, artistic, marketing, sales and other types of work.

HomeBasedWork
http://www.homebasedwork.com/
HomeBasedWork provides a variety of tips, articles and resources to help you begin at work at home career. Among these is the *At Home Workers Express*, a monthly newsletter designed for everyone who has ever wanted to work from home. Whether you want to work for a company offering home-based work, or you want to start your own home-based business, you will find plenty of useful tips to help you

Looking for freelance work..

HomeBasedWork 🏠 com

Helping you join the work at home revolution

Home | Working for an Employer | Working for Yourself | Products & Resources
Home Based Opportunities | Articles Library | Advertise | Contact

Working from home can be a very rewarding experience. In recent years, it has become more and more popular as an alternative means of employment.

HomeBasedWork.com provides a variety of tips, articles, and resources to help you begin at work at home career. Some people may prefer working for an employer rather than starting a business of their own; regardless of what you choose, **you** are the only one that can make it happen!

Subscribe to the At Home Workers Express Ezine

Tired of being swindled and scammed? Just want an honest way to make money from home? The At Home Workers Express is a monthly publication that can help you to find the telecommuting job or business opportunity that you've been

Featured Sponsor

Small Business Owner Survey

I WANT A PHONE NUMBER THAT GIVES ME:

- FREE VOICEMAIL OVER THE INTERNET AND PHONE
- MY OWN 800# FOR LIFE
- 5¢ A MINUTE CALLING

No monthly fees or hidden charges. Only pay for the services you use! Get 100 free minutes when you sign up!

Fig. 14. The web site of Home Based Work.

start your work at home career. You will also find reviews of various home business opportunities. For a free subscription you can enter your email address and click the Join List button.

Jobsunlimited
http://www.jobsunlimited.co.uk/
You can search for freelance work in the *Guardian* and *Observer* newspapers via this site.

Outsource 2000
http://outsource2000.com
OutSource2000 has joined forces with the leading sources in the home-based work related industry to create an online forum where individuals throughout the north America and the rest of the world can now get continuously updated information relating to 'all aspects' of working from home. They say: 'Inside our Home Workers Forum is an unparalleled selection of home-based jobs and opportunities, over 50 separate job search databases, and everything else needed to make your future as a home-based worker complete.' Out-Source2000 has been developing home-based work related programs, products, and services since 1993.

Recruit Media
http://www.recruitmedia.co.uk
This service is aimed at creative and technical people working on either a freelance or permanent basis. Established since 1989, Recruit Media is a member of FRES, the UK Federation of Recruitment & Employment Services.

Refer

http://www.refer.com/

This web site offers two main ways to make money. First, you can take your pick from the range of freelance jobs on offer, and second you can earn referral fees for recommending friends and colleagues. They say: 'With more than 75,000 job openings, refer.com is the best job referral site designed for people who are natural networkers with an ability to match jobs with candidates. The service is free, completely confidential, and holds no risk or obligation for you or the people you contact.'

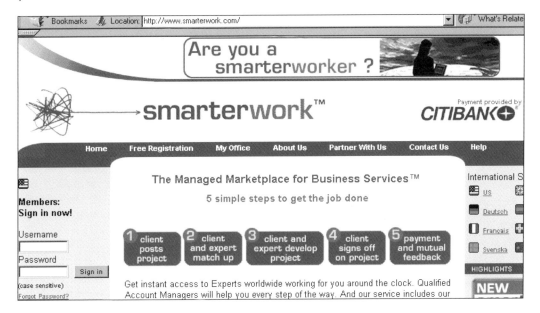

Smarterwork

http://www.smarterwork.com/

You can get the job done – 100 per cent online. Smarterwork describes itself as the complete virtual office. You will find the right people, a secure environment, and all the tools you need to work with others on projects. And the global payment system ensures that you really can do business with people all over the world. Freelance work includes writing, editing, graphic design, web build support, and document production. The site includes special sections on start-ups and small/medium businesses.

TalentX

http://www.talentx.com/

If you're a graphic designer, illustrator, photographer or fine artist, TalentX provides an opportunity for you to showcase your work to a global audience. All your works are protected by Viewguard technology, so that prospective clients can view your work, but they cannot save it to disk. Work is also protected by a floating watermark, while

Fig. 15. The web site of Smarter Work.

online contracts with buyers safeguard your rights. Using TalentX offers a number of benefits, including the ability to create a digital portfolio and tailor it for client meetings, sell your digital stock and earn extra revenues online, gain commissions from corporate buyers and agencies, and interact with other creative professionals.

UK Business Net
http://www.uk-business.net/
The site offers a range of classified advertisements for business opportunities, trade leads, franchises, and more. The main categories of advertising are: UK business opportunities, trade leads and business services, international business opportunities, import/export, brokers, agents and representatives, miscellaneous, finance and loans, stock and merchandise, businesses for sale, franchises, commercial property, real estate, professional services, invention marketing, wholesalers and retailers, multi-level marketing (MLM), and employment opportunities.

Vault
http://www.vault.com/
Vault is an email-based job search and job matching service. It also sells industry guides, employer profiles and insider research, and runs various message boards. As well as offering a wealth of free jobs information and career advice, it also has a whole channel devoted to freelancing, and hosts a busy freelance marketplace.

Wholesaler UK
http://www.thewholesaler.co.uk/html/internet_opportunities.html
This site has a section on internet-related business opportunities.

Work Exchange
http://www.workexchange.com
This is a marketplace for employers and freelancers looking for project-oriented work. Once employers post a contract project, the site searches its extensive database of freelance professionals to find the best match. It includes a useful guide to establishing an internet presence in ten easy steps. The service is a division of Lycos, the search engine and portal site.

Associations for freelancers

Independent Homeworkers Alliance
http://www.homeworkers.org/
The IHA says it is a membership-driven organisation dedicated to help the success of those who telecommute from the home-based workplace. Telecommuters, short-term contract workers, and people wishing to make a home-based career can all use the employment resources found here. All membership and maintenance fees are ap-

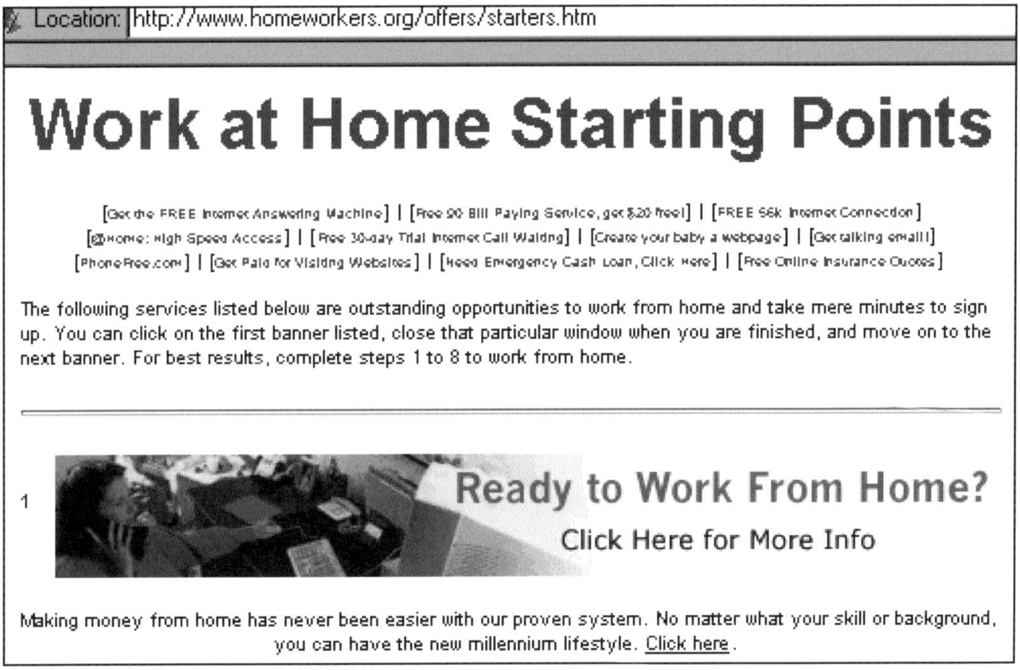

Location: http://www.homeworkers.org/offers/starters.htm

Work at Home Starting Points

[Get the FREE Internet Answering Machine] | [Free 2¢ Bill Paying Service, get $20 free!] | [FREE 56k Internet Connection]
[@Home: High Speed Access] | [Free 30-day Trial Internet Call Waiting] | [Create your baby a webpage!] | [Get talking email!]
[PhoneFree.com] | [Get Paid for Visiting Websites] | [Need Emergency Cash Loan, Click Here] | [Free Online Insurance Quotes]

The following services listed below are outstanding opportunities to work from home and take mere minutes to sign up. You can click on the first banner listed, close that particular window when you are finished, and move on to the next banner. For best results, complete steps 1 to 8 to work from home.

1   **Ready to Work From Home?**
     Click Here for More Info

Making money from home has never been easier with our proven system. No matter what your skill or background, you can have the new millennium lifestyle. Click here.

plied directly to the membership to improve, enhance, and add to the advantages, benefits and services provided to all members. The IHA has over 30,000 members. They are self-employed, skilled and unskilled, full and part-time professionals, and telecommuters, along with those who have already established a home-based office. There are over 13,000 assignments in its database. It offers all members benefits that are designed specifically for the home worker. Jobs encompass a wide variety of fields and disciplines, from medical transcription and writing to mystery shopping and programming and more.

Fig. 16. The Independent Homeworkers Alliance (IHA) has set up a web site.

More Internet Handbooks to help you

Finding a Job on the Internet, Brendan Murphy (2nd edition).
Where to Find It on the Internet, Kye Valongo (2nd edition).

4 Marketing the home-based business

In this chapter we will explore:

▶ *advertising and media*
▶ *contacting businesses*
▶ *marketing in Usenet newsgroups*
▶ *marketing advice on the world wide web*
▶ *marketing associations*

. . . .

How this chapter can help you

This chapter describes web sites which can help you:

1. Find programs that generate full postal addresses from only the postcode.

2. Browse through market research reference books for entrepreneurs.

3. Take advantage of business information services for home workers.

4. Learn how to make money using the internet secrets of top web marketeers.

5. Access a directory of 1.6 million-plus classified businesses around the UK.

6. Explore American press and media by state.

7. Find a directory of UK media sites on the internet.

8. Find listings of newspapers and magazines for the US and the rest of the world.

Advertising and media

Advertising Standards Authority
http://www.asa.org.uk/
The ASA aims to promote the highest standards in advertising. It does this by a programme of industry information and training through some 70 presentations and seminars each year. It actively promotes its work and role through a co-ordinated media relations strategy to the advertising industry and consumers.

All Newspapers
http://www.allnewspapers.com
The site offers hyperlinks to top stories and to local, national, and international newspapers, magazines, electronic media, and news agencies.

Audit Bureau of Circulation
http://www.abc.org.uk
ABC is home to over 3,300 national and international titles, and is an authoritative source of the circulation figures of periodicals of every kind. They say: 'Through continued re-investment of profits into improving effectiveness, the ABC audit will continue to ensure full disclosure, simplicity and comparability of data, for the benefit of media owners, advertising agencies and advertisers worldwide.'

E&P Directory of Online Newspapers
http://www.mediainfo.com/emedia/
This is a substantial database of newspapers and radio stations from all over the world. It includes a range of clearly set out search functions and listings to get you started. The database contains over 12,000 records – well worth checking out.

Fig. 17. The E&P Directory provides handy links to thousands of online newspapers and magazines from around the world.

Ecola's Newsstand Directory
http://www.ecola.com/news/press/
Logically organized links provide easy access to periodicals world-

wide. Over 8,400 newspapers and magazines are listed, all of which are maintained by a paper-printed publication, and which provide English language content online. Recommended.

Electronic Newsstand
http://www.image.dk/~knud-sor/en/
This enterprising resource contains links to a vast number and variety of international news sources, supported by quick reference regional maps. Definitely worth exploring.

Gebbie Press
http://www.gebbieinc.com/presto.htm
This American site offers free resources and access to press and media by state.

Hollis UK Press and Public Relations Annual
http://www.hollis-pr.co.uk
Hollis is a well-known UK publisher of media reference guides. On its web site you can link into publications, PR consultancies, contacts and services.

Marketing and Creative Handbook
http://www.mch.co.uk/
Here you will find a useful set of online directories covering advertising, design, marketing and publicity in Great Britain. You can search for information on a national or regional basis.

Media UK Directory
http://www.mediauk.com/directory/
This site offers a useful directory of UK media sites on the internet.

News Directory
http://www.newsdirectory.com/
The site contains over 17,000 categorised information links.

Newslink
http://ajr.newslink.org/news.html
Here you can find listings of newspapers and magazines for the United States and the rest of the world. You can use the information for advertising, and for mailing out press releases.

Periodical Publishers Association
http://www.ppa.co.uk
The PPA is the umbrella organisation for magazine publishers in the UK. Its site includes a comprehensive list of UK magazines which have web sites.

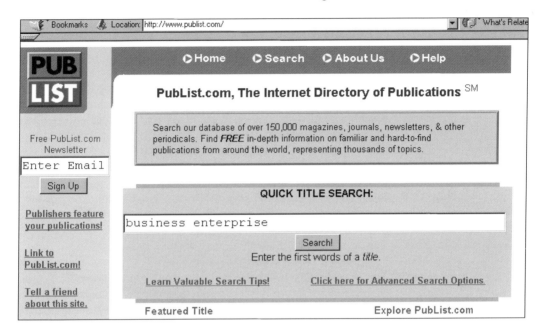

PubList

http://www.publist.com

PubList.com is a massive internet-based reference for over 150,000 domestic and international print and electronic publications. These include magazines, journals, e-journals, newsletters, and mono- graphs. It provides quick and easy access to detailed publication information including, titles, formats, publisher addresses, editor con- tacts, circulation data, and ISSN numbers. The site also provides access to subscription services as well as article level information through rights and permissions providers and document delivery ser- vices.

Fig. 18. PubList is a major internet-based reference source covering more than 150,000 domestic and international print and electronic publications.

Contacting businesses

AFD Postcodes and ADF ZipAddresses

http://www.afd.co.uk (postcode information)

http://www.zipaddress.com (zip address information)

These two programs use software that generates full addresses from only the postcode – you just add the street number or house name. The PostCode version covers the UK. ZipAddress covers all the US zipcodes with more than 100 million addresses. It also has a built-in one-off label printing facility and a PostNet barcode font.

Amazon.co.uk

http://www.amazon.co.uk

With more than a million book titles on its database, the Amazon online bookshop offers a comprehensive list of market research re- ference books for the entrepreneur.

Marketing the home-based business ....

Ask Alix
http://askalix.co.uk/
This is a directory of 1.8 million UK companies. You can search by keyword, name or town. The system is currently servicing over 10,000 searches and directory look-ups per hour. You can advertise your general goods and services, motor cars, or property and insert personal ads free of charge. Each ad without an email address can utilise Alex's free drop-a-note feature, for confidential contact between advertisers and customers. Advertisers can also extend the life of their ads and hot-link them to their own web site. AskAlex was designed, written and implemented by Miami International Ltd which, despite its exotic sounding name, is based in Stockton-on-Tees.

Big Book USA
http://www.bigbook.com
This is a fantastic web site that puts basic information about more than 11 million US businesses at your fingertips. Each Big Book listing provides the company's name, an industry category, address, city, state, zip code, phone number, and street map location. In the classifieds section you can search ads, create ads, and edit ads. It is owned by GTE, one of the largest publicly owned telecommunications companies in the world.

Big Yellow Pages
http://www.bigyellow.com/
Big Yellow offers a huge coverage of some 11 million business listings in the USA. You can search this massive directory by state, business type, address, and name. You can add your personal and business names to the database. The site includes a very helpful set of FAQs. The site is a service of Bell Atlantic.

Big Yellow Pages – World
http://www.bigyellow.com/g_home.html
This is a substantial compilation of yellow page directories from around the world. It has also links to news, travel and weather information. To begin your search for the directory you are looking for, just click on a colour map of the world for the continent you require.

BT Directory Enquiries
http://www.bt.com/phonenetuk/
On this page you can enter the name of the business or person you are looking for and the area in which they reside, then press the relevant search button to quickly get their phone number (unless it is ex-directory) There are some helpful FAQs to help you if you get stuck. For example: 'Business names may be listed in a number of ways If you were unable to find Jones, Smith & Brown Ltd it may be because they are listed as JSB Limited, or perhaps J.S.B. Limited.

Another possibility is that the business trades under a different name from that listed in the phone book.'

BT Number Change
http://www.numberchange.bt.com
Are you using the new national dialling codes? The old numbers will soon no longer work (the date of the final changeover differs for each area). You can sign up here for a reminder service to help you plan for the remaining changes. You can spread the word about your new number with a customised e-postcard, get advice on getting your print work altered for the Big Number, obtain a summary of its many downloads on the BT big number site, and even download a version of this site for your company intranet, or have your own portable Big Number web site.

Business Database
http://www.ypbd.co.uk
The Business Database from Yellow Pages is a UK leader in location-based data. With more than 11 years' experience in the direct marketing industry, it has helped thousands of companies to generate new business leads. It claims to be the UK's largest and most comprehensive single source of location based business information, with some 1.7 million UK businesses listed. They say: 'Register today, select your target market and let us give you a count on your potential customers and show how little it costs to generate new leads and hit your sales targets.'

Business Telephone Numbers
http://www.192enquiries.com
From this very handy and easy to use page, you can search for the phone numbers of over 2.1 million UK businesses and organisations. With a permanent in-house verification team, they say that every entry is researched in person, without exception. Some 65,000 calls are made every week to validate and update entries. Businesses and organisations have the facility to update their entries online, instantly and free anywhere in the world.

BusinessZone
http://www.businesszone.co.uk/
This site provides a business information service for home workers and small to medium enterprises providing access to real-time news, company and market research data as well as an accountancy directory and discussion forum.

Companies Online
http://www.companiesonline.com/
Here you will find an authoritative Dun and Bradstreet/Lycos directory of US companies. You can search by state, city, industry, and

company name. The site also offers links to company web sites.

Datagold
http://www.datagold.com/
On this British-run web site, you can find listings of UK companies, searchable by geographic location. Datagold titles include the UK Training Directory, UK Recruitment Directory, UK Marketing Directory (actually wider, including PR, Market Research etc), the UK Export Directory, UK Accountants Directory, UK Management Consultants Directory and the UK Internet Service Provider Directory.

Electronic Yellow Pages
http://www.eyp.co.uk
EYP links you to classified business listings in the UK. The web site gives you access to *Yellow Pages*, the UK's top classified commercial directory, and to *Business Pages*, one of the UK's top business-to-business directories. You can also access *Talking Pages*, the UK's leading classified telephone information service, *YELL*, the web site from Yellow Pages, the *Business Database*, a definitive UK business data source, and *Message Services,* for communication links. EYP is a division of British Telecommunications plc.

In Business
http://www.inbusiness.co.uk/
This is a comprehensive online directory of 2 million businesses in Britain from Thomson Directories, a company which has produced yellow pages directories for many years. You can search by company, product and location. It provides a limited amount of local information. They say that details are checked and verified on average every 12 to 18 months. If they cannot contact anyone at the listed business number the entry is removed.

International Business Lists
http://www.iblists.co.uk
IBL is a UK-based provider of business mailing lists. It was established in 1995 as the list rental division of the Metal Bulletin plc group of companies. IBL provides up-to-date contact names and addresses of decision making business professionals involved in financial derivatives, metals, industrial minerals, energy, shipping and mining. It can provide mailing lists to parallel the needs of any direct marketing campaign targeting decision-makers around the world – in any of these multi-billion pound industries.

Internet Directory Enquiries
http://www.internet192.com/
Over 1.4 million listings can be accessed through this site which includes an A to Z of business categories. You can search for businesses by region.

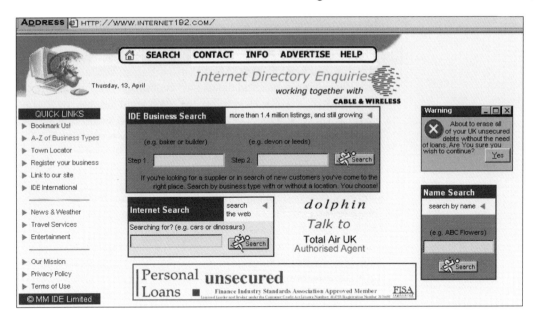

Fig. 19. Internet Directory Enquiries. With around 1.4 million listings you stand a good chance of finding the person or organisation you want.

Internet Pages

http://the-internet-pages.co.uk

Internet Pages promotes access to businesses throughout the UK. It covers everything from local builders to mechanics and carpet cleaners.

Kellys Directories

http://www.kellys.co.uk

This is a long-established directory of around 12,000 leading companies in the UK, giving contact details. Registration (free) is required before you can access any part of the site.

Scoot

http://www.scoot.co.uk

Based in Oxford and London, Scoot offers a fast and friendly approach to finding information. Whatever you need to know, you can call free on 0800 192 192. It can give information about a large number of UK businesses and services, 24 hours a day, 365 days a year. Free Pages was set up in 1992 to provide electronic directory services to UK and European markets. You can search through 1.6 million records (this number is growing rapidly), with over 3,000 business categories and 27,000 locations in its database; you can search either by name or by location and sector. There is also Scoot Holland and Scoot Belgium. You can subscribe your business to Scoot, which it says is seeking to establish a lead in dial-up information services. You can add your business details to its database by filling in the submission form.

Telephone Directories on the Web
http://www.teldir.com/
This site claims to be the internet's original and most detailed index of online phone books, with links to yellow pages, white pages, business directories, email addresses and fax listings from all around the world. Telephone Directories on the Web was created by Robert Hoare in 1995, and has been frequently updated since. This site apparently now gets more than half a million page views every month.

Thomson Directories INbusiness
http://www.inbusiness.co.uk
A comprehensive online directory of businesses in Britain can be found here.

Thomson Directories Online
http://www.thomweb.org.uk
http://www.thomson-directories.co.uk/
Thomson Yellow Pages introduced Yellow Pages to the UK in 1966 as sales agents for the Post Office. In 1980 the company recognised a need in the local marketplace for a local directory. Thomson Directories Ltd set up as an independent directory publisher and piloted local directories in six regions. National rollout of the Thomson Local followed in 1981. Today Thomson Directories delivers information products using its regularly updated database of more than two million business listings. On this site you will find full details of ThomWeb, The Thomson Local, Business Search UK CD ROM, Business Search Pro CD-rom, New Connections and the Thomson Database.

US Business Park Company Search Facility
http://www.andybri.demon.co.uk/
Hundreds of company links can be found here.

UK Pages
http://www.ukpages.co.uk/
UK Pages is an extensive internet directory listing of businesses across England, Scotland, Northern Ireland and Wales, with direct links to web sites. It provides a free entry for all businesses in the UK and includes up to four free specialist category headings.

UKPlus
http://www.ukplus.co.uk/
UKPlus is an annotated, searchable directory of UK web sites, designed to help you find what you want, quickly and easily. It has built a vast store of web site reviews compiled by a team of journalists. Although it concentrates on UK web sites of all kinds, it includes many from all over the world which are likely to be of interest to British-based readers. In reviewing each new web site it seeks to exclude offensive material. The parent company of UK Plus is Daily

Mail & General Trust — owners of *The Daily Mail, The Mail on Sunday, London Evening Standard* and various UK regional newspapers.

UK Web Directory
http://www.ukdirectory.com/
This directory lists over 15,000 UK web sites, grouped by sector. It also maintains a section for personal home pages. UK Directory offers one free basic listing to all web sites originating in the United Kingdom. Professional banner advertising can help build your site traffic and several packages are now available for web sites wishing to target a predominantly UK market.

World Pages
http://www.worldpages.com/
World Pages is an internet business directory which offers direct access to 112 million US and Canadian white and yellow pages listings, 9 million email addresses, 30 million URLs, and links to over 200 directories world wide.

Yellow Pages Directory
http://uk.yell.com/home.html

Marketing — Usenet newsgroups

Newsgroups are public discussion groups freely available on the internet. Each newsgroup is a collection of messages, usually unedited and not checked by anyone ('unmoderated'). Messages can be posted in the newsgroup by anyone including you. The ever-growing newsgroups have been around for much longer than the world wide web and web pages, and are an endless source of information, news, scandal, entertainment, resources and ideas. The 80,000-plus newsgroups are collectively referred to as Usenet. To access newsgroups, you will need a news reader, a type of software that enables you to search, read, post and manage messages in a newsgroup. It will normally be supplied as part of your internet service when you first sign up, e.g. Internet Explorer/Outlook, or Netscape/Messenger.

Advertising on Usenet
http://www.danger.com/advo.html
How to do it, how not to do it — an explanation of why indiscriminate advertising in Usenet is frowned upon. This site suggests ways in which those who wish to advertise in Usenet newsgroups can do so constructively and without causing offence.

Deja.com
http://www.deja.com/
Deja.com (originally Deja News) was founded in 1995 to give people a way of accessing newsgroups using their web browser such as Internet Explorer or Netscape Navigator (rather than a newsreader

Marketing the home-based business ....

Fig. 20. An example of a Usenet newsgroup concerned with marketing matters. Anyone can read and post messages in such newsgroups including you.

such as Outlook Express or Netscape Messenger). With more than six million page views per day, Deja offers access to more than 45,000 newsgroups and is one of the web's most visited sites. More than a million people have registered (free) to take advantage of its expanding range of information and community services.

News:alt.www.marketing

This is an example of a Usenet newsgroup dedicated to marketing issues. You might be able to pick up some useful ideas here from other net marketers.

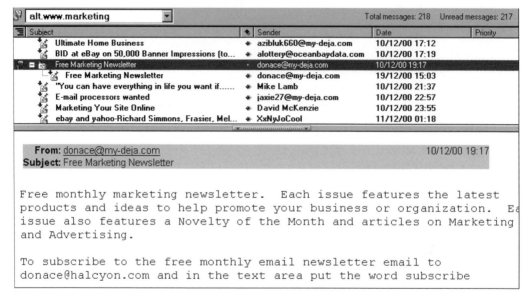

Marketing advice on the world wide web

Complete Internet Marketing
http://members.spree.com/business/martrade/
Learn how to make money by taking advantage of the internet secrets of some top web marketeers.

Franchise Business
http://www.lds.co.uk/franchise/
Published by The Franchise Business in Poole, Dorset, this site includes information about UK franchise opportunities, and provides details of specialist lawyers and consultants. If you are considering the purchase of a franchise, or seeking advice and assistance regarding the franchising of an existing business, these pages will prove a useful source of information.

Franinfo.co.uk
http://www.franinfo.co.uk
Franinfo describes itself as the UK's most comprehensive directory of

franchises with essential information for franchisees and franchisors. It includes useful links to all the key organisations, trade associations and media in the UK franchising industry.

Free Well at Icemall
http://www.icemall.com/free/free_marketing.html
This site offers free marketing tips and reports, web marketing and search engine tactics, a free internet marketing report, free internet marketing tips, and internet marketing software with a trial download.

Freepromo.cjb.net
http://freepromo.cjb.net
Invites you to learn how to promote your site here.

Imarketing Services
http://www.imarketingservices.co.uk
This is the web site of Sara Edlington, the UK internet marketing consultant, former marketing consultant for Demon Internet, and author of another title in the Internet Handbooks series, *Marketing Your Business on the Internet*, now in a second edition. Details of a free newsletter can be found here, together with a resource centre on business building on the internet.

Internet Advertising Resource Guide
http://www.admedia.org/
This well documented site offers a very useful information resource for internet marketing and advertising. It contains a huge number of marketing-related links intelligently categorised under main headings including introduction, planning, development, management, research and teaching. The site is an ongoing project of Dr Hairong Li, an Assistant Professor in the Department of Advertising at Michigan State University.

Internet Magazine – Marketing Hot List
http://www.internet-magazine.com/hot/
This EMAP publication contains some valuable marketing background and pointers including UK market overview, market size, UK and world user demographics, and attitudes. Here you can sort out fact from fiction among the statistics about internet usage world wide. The Hot List includes also includes timely and authoritative information about the UK, Europe's hottest internet marketplace.

Internet Marketing Tips
http://www.marketingtips.com/
The site offers tips, strategies, and secrets for internet marketing, online advertising, and web site promotion for the small business or office. You can subscribe to the monthly *Internet Marketing Tips Newsletter* with hundreds of promotional tips and tricks, free online.

Marketing the home-based business ....

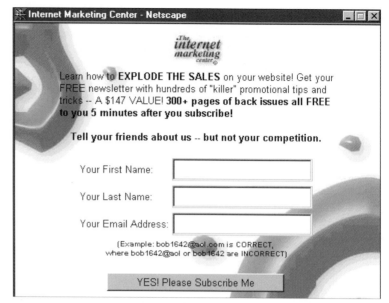

Fig. 21. You could pick up lots of useful advice and contacts by subscribing to an online marketing magazine such as this one published by Marketing Tips.

Marketing Tips

http://www.marketingtips.com/tipsltr.html

This site brings an aggressive approach to all aspects of internet marketing. You can find out about web page promotion and design, online services, online classified ads, newsgroup promotions, promotions through discussion lists and newsletters. There is also information on bulk email, auto responders, bulletin boards, electronic malls, ranking at the top of search engines, sales strategies, creating killer copy, banner ads (tips and tricks), and completely automating your business. You can subscribe to the monthly *Internet Marketing Tips* newsletter, with hundreds of promotional tips and tricks, free online.

Marketing UK

http://www.marketinguk.co.uk

Here is another very useful site for UK marketing information and advice, which aims to help marketing executives to be more effective. It deals with everything from the basics of marketing to setting up a web site, with links to best practice, books and magazines, marketing training, planning, marketing checklists, contact databases, public relations, using the internet, internet services, your own site, ten-point strategy, and check your site.

MINTEL Market Research

http://www.mintel.com

You can access instant purchasing and viewing of consumer research online via this home page.

Promotion World
http://www.promotionworld.com/
This site has all the free information on promoting your web site you may ever need. There are hundreds of articles, interviews, and other features and resources. The site includes a 40 page tutorial covering many of the basic aspects of promotion, plus interviews with some well known internet promotion and marketing experts.

Small & Medium-sized Enterprises UK
http://uk.sme.com/
SME World Wide is dedicated to the small and medium sized enterprises of the world. This is its UK section, which contains a selection of basic business links including those to national and governmental organisations.

The Biz – Marketing
http://www.thebiz.co.uk/mar.htm
The Biz is a useful UK business web sites directory. Its marketing section provides a useful gateway to a whole range of marketing data, products and services for above and below the line as well as creative services, venues and exhibitions. The marketing section covers advertising agencies, associations, professional bodies, audio-visual production, broadcast media, conferences, exhibitions, consumer marketing, corporate hospitality, data processing agencies, direct marketing agencies, field marketing, franchises, fulfilment, graphic design consultants, illustrators, mailing list brokers, market research agencies, photographers, print, print media, product designers, promotional gifts, public relations agencies, publishing agencies, sponsorship consultants, translation agencies, and venues.

UK Business Net
http://www.ukbusinessnet.com/
The UK Business Net aims to be a comprehensive business-to-business information resource and marketing forum. This site is dedicated to the needs of companies operating in the UK business-to-business marketplace – including their promotion to overseas organisations. It contains some 4,000 pages of free-access information on financial markets, trade news, forthcoming industrial and commercial events, trade and technical media, internet resources and more. The UK Companies Database is the latest major addition to its site. It contains contact details for organisations operating in the UK business-to-business marketplace with an established internet presence. If your company operates in the business-to-business sector you are invited to take advantage of this service.

Webring.org
http://www.webring.org
A web ring is a network of web sites with a common interest, and

Marketing the home-based business ....

Fig. 22. Webring is a huge and diverse network of interlinked web sites. It has recently been acquired by the internet directory, Yahoo!.

which link in to each other. This free service at Webring.org offers easy access to hundreds of thousands of member web sites organised by related interests. You can find rings that interest you by clicking on topics in the subject directory or by using the search box. Web Ring is one of the simplest and most efficient ways to find content on the internet. Its member sites are everywhere. Anytime you find yourself at a Web Ring member page, just click on the navigation buttons or hypertext to travel to other sites in the ring. Any web site owner can apply to join an existing ring or create a new ring. Rings are listed in the directory once they contain at least five sites.

Wilson Web
http://www.wilsonweb.com
This established and worthwhile resource contains a mass of information about doing business on the net. It contains literally hundreds of articles, and more than 2,000 links to resources on ecommerce and web marketing. It has organised the practice of online selling into more than 40 helpful categories, and grouped materials within these topics for quick reference.

Marketing associations

Chartered Institute of Marketing
http://www.cim.co.uk/
With more than 60,000 members, the CIM is the world's largest marketing association. It works closely with the marketing profession, government, industry and commerce to promote awareness and understanding of what marketing can contribute to UK and international business. The CIM also operates a comprehensive information service and a mail order publications service.

Direct Marketing Association
http://www.dma.org.uk
The DMA is the core trade organisation for all companies in direct marketing in the UK. Formed in 1992, its aim is to promote and protect the direct marketing industry. Membership includes advertisers from a broad range of business sectors, direct marketing and telemarketing agencies, and service suppliers from printers and mailing houses to list brokers and database consultancies.

Direct Electronic Mail Marketing Association
http://www.memo.net/demma/dema.html
DEMM offers consumers the facility for getting off email lists, as well as listing those they can join. Try some out to see how email marketing is being done.

Electronic Commerce Association
http://www.eca.org.uk/
The ECA is a leading UK centre of electronic commerce expertise and experience. It promotes the use of electronic commerce by providing independent help, guidance, information and advice representing members' interests. It provides a forum for the exchange of experience and the development of best practice. It aims to encourage improvements in industrial, commercial and governmental efficiency by offering guidance and practical solutions to enable organisations make the most effective use of electronic commerce.

Federation of Small Businesses
http://www.fsb.org.uk
With some 130,000 members, the FSB is a non-political organisation formed to help small businesses. It urges all political parties to help reduce the burdens on business, to tackle the problem of late payment, and improve incentives for businesses thereby enabling them to expand their enterprise. FSB members enjoy a range of benefits including a legal advice line as well as information on tax, VAT and health and safety issues. It also offers special insurance against legal and professional fees, employment disputes, jury service, criminal prosecutions, and other contingencies. It publishes a regular magazine for members; and regional branches hold regular meetings for members. The site includes an online membership enquiry form.

Forum of Private Business
http://www.fpb.co.uk
Now in its 21st year, the FPB helps small and medium-sized enterprises (SMEs) to succeed by fighting for their interests in the UK and Europe, and by delivering high quality information and new products to promote self-reliance, efficiency, and profitability.

Free FSB Newsletter

E-MAIL

Join our growing army of members subscribing to our email newsletter Get the the latest small business news delivered directly to your desk!

Marketing the home-based business ....

Bookmarks   Location: http://www.isbc.com/isbc/   What'

International Small Business **Consortium**
**Helping small business spend the least amount
of time and money to maximize the Internet.**

Database

▶ Search or Update
▶ Join or Register (it's free)

Services

▶ Mission and Goals
▶ Business Discussion Group
▶ Marketing Tips
▶ The Life of a Small
     Business Owner
▶ Business Issues
▶ Useful Business Sites
▶ Internet Survey
▶ Learn from Mistakes

Helping Businesses Make Connections

▶ **33,000+ Member Businesses**
▶ **In 140+ Countries**

ISBC is an Internet Based Resource Serving:

▶ **SMEs - Small and Medium-Sized Enterprises**
▶ **Small Businesses**
▶ **SOHOs**

In the areas of:

▶ **Locating Business Assistance.**

Fig. 23. The home page
of the International Small
Business Consortium.

International Small Business Consortium
http://www.isbc.com
The ISBC offers a productive and professional internet/web based
network to help SMEs communicate about business needs, expand
their markets, share their resources, knowledge and experience. It
seeks to furnish one reference source for business information, resources and experts from around the world, and protected from
non-productive and meaningless side issues. This sensible and well
organised site provides help in the areas of locating business assistance, helping develop and establish useful international business
connections, offering business links, publishing a business newsletter, and providing information and news on business issues of
interest. All ISBC services are free to the users.

More Internet Handbooks to help you

Marketing Your Business on the Internet, Sara Edlington (2nd edition)
Naming a Web Site on the Internet, Graham Jones
Promoting a Web Site on the Internet, Graham Jones

5 Financial matters

In this chapter we will explore:

▶ *accountancy and book-keeping services*
▶ *UK bank web sites*
▶ *sources of business finance*
▶ *financial services and information*
▶ *insurance*
▶ *taxation and regulation*

How this chapter can help you

This chapter describes web sites which can help you:

1. Locate qualified accountants in your area to help you with book-keeping and tax advice.

2. Discover which banks are now online.

3. Explore possible business grants and venture capital from private and public sources.

4. Enhance your corporate image with personalised cheques.

5. View some easy-to-use bookkeeping software.

6. Explore some of the leading UK-based web site directories for financial services.

7. Obtain a guaranteed bank loan through the DTI.

8. Obtain a personal financial appraisal.

9. Check out the latest trends in the online banking industry.

10. Find out about the Inland Revenue and self assessment.

11. Explore a credit and consumer debt advice online.

12. Access business insurance for home workers.

Accountancy and book-keeping services

Association of Chartered Certified Accountants
http://www.acca.co.uk
Equipped with financial, business and strategic skills, ACCA members in practice can provide the full range of accounting services. In many cases they are also available to act as non-executive directors or business mentors. The Association provides a database of Members

who are available to act as non-executive directors, as well as advice on choosing a qualified accountant in your local area.

DO$H book-keeping
http://www.dosh.co.uk
DO$H Cashbook assumes no book-keeping knowledge and provides help through on-screen steps and a comprehensive manual. The software allows users to produce a complete record of all their receipts and payments, a cash flow summary, a VAT account, and bank reconciliation statements for any period and prints reports on to A4 paper.

Institute of Chartered Accountants of England & Wales
http://www.icaew.co.uk
The ICAEW is the senior professional accountancy organisation for England and Wales. Its members often act as auditors of company and other business accounts, and are entitled to place the letters ACA or FCA after their name. The Institute has over 118,000 members. They work in all areas of business, all around the world. Qualifying as a chartered accountant requires individuals to pass rigorous professional exams and to complete a training contract. All Chartered Accountants are governed by the same ethical code and the Institute seeks to ensure that they adhere to these high professional standards.

Fig. 24. You can use the web site of the Institute of Chartered Accountants of England & Wales to contact an accountant or partnership in your local area.

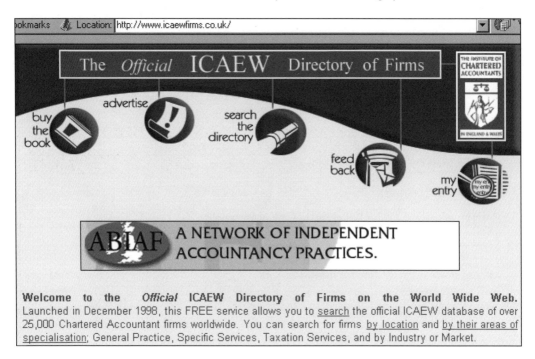

Institute of Chartered Accountants of Scotland
http://www.icas.org.uk/
Like its professional colleagues south of the border, ICAS's members

provide a variety of accountancy, auditing, tax and advisory services for business clients.

The MacDonald Partnership
http://www.tmp.co.uk
This firm of chartered accountants people has produced a Windows compatible disk called *The A – Z of Rescue and Insolvency* which is designed as a guide to all options available in case the worst happens in your business career – possible insolvency. You can also download material from their web site. It is free to anyone on request. TMP specialises in organising Voluntary Arrangements for companies, individuals and partnerships in which debtors agree to pay off debts – fully or partially – usually over a period of 3 to 5 years, as an alternative to bankruptcy or liquidation.

UK bank web sites

Abbey National
http://www.abbeynational.co.uk

Alliance & Leicester
http://www.alliance-leicester.co.uk

Bank of England
http://www.bankofengland.co.uk

Bank of Scotland
http://www.bankofscotland.co.uk

Fig. 25. The Bank of Scotland web site. From electronic banking to business banking, everything you need is just a click away.

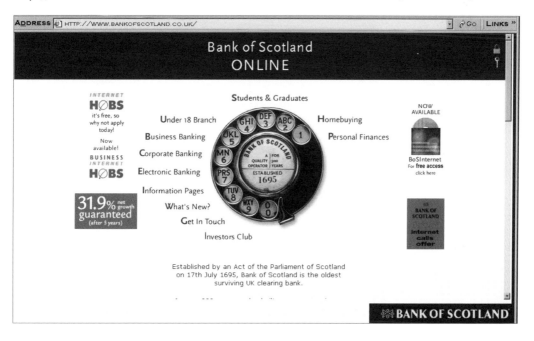

Financial matters...

Barclays Bank Online
http://www.barclays.co.uk/online

Co-operative Bank
http://www.co-operativebank.co.uk

Egg (Prudential Corporation)
http://www.egg.com

Fig. 26. You can take care of all your financial needs entirely online with the innovative Egg service, courtesy of the Prudential insurance and personal finance group.

First-e
http://www.first-e.com
This is an internet-only bank.

Halifax
http://www.halifax.co.uk

HSBC Bank
http://www.hsbc.co.uk

LloydsTSB
http://www.lloydstsb.co.uk

NatWest
http://www.natwest.co.uk

Sources of business finance

Your own high street bank may be the best starting point in your search for business finance, whether in the form of an overdraft facility, or longer-term finance for plant and equipment. It may also be able to help you with advice and suggestions for other forms of finance, grants and loans. However, here are some more specialist web sites which may be able to help you:

3i
http://www.3i.com
Quite a large number of venture capital companies have experience in putting up capital for internet start-up businesses. Backed and funded by major British financial institutions, the established firm of 3i ('investors in industry') is one of the biggest venture capital organisations in Europe, with enormous experience of helping small and medium sized enterprises to grow.

Best Grants Database in Britain
http://www.enterprise.net/cds/grants/
This one-page site offers a database of UK and European Union business grants which is in use in over 200 colleges and universities in the UK. The database contains details of over 300 grants from the European Union plus over 1,000 other grants available from the UK government, plus details of grants paid by Training and Enterprise Councils, and local authorities. There is a separate grants database for Scotland. The latest addition to the database is details of over 200 grants from major trusts and grants available for community development. The grants database forms a useful resource for training organisations, colleges, universities, schools and Enterprise Agencies.

British Venture Capital Association
http://www.bvca.co.uk
This association represents the top players in the venture capital industry. Its web site features various downloadable documents in PDF format including information about that informal source of venture capital, so-called business angels (private investors with cash to spare).

CORDIS
http://www.cordis.lu
CORDIS stands for the Community Research and Development Information Service. Based in Luxembourg, it provides a useful source of information about European R&D programmes. It could for example help you take part in EU-funded research programmes, identify possible business partners, transfer your innovative ideas, and boost your business. The site can be viewed in several different languages.

Crescendo Ventures
http://www.crescendoventures.com
This is the site of an international venture-capital organisation specialising in 'early-stage investment opportunities in the communications and eBusiness fields'. It has offices in the UK (London) and the US (Minneapolis in Minnesota, and Palo Alto in California).

EU Information Society Projects
http://www.ukishelp.co.uk
There are excellent new opportunities for UK organisations to obtain funding from the European Union for innovative development and application projects involving IT, multimedia, telecoms, broadcasting and electronic commerce. 1999 saw the start of a new funding programme called Framework 5. If you are unfamiliar with EC-funded R&D, read the site's guide. There are also other IS-related programmes which run concurrently with Framework 5. See the Sources of Funds section for more information.

Four Leaf
http://www.fourleaf.com
Fourleaf aims to bring together internet startups, companies, investors and their professional advisers. DealBase – its online database of deals and dealmakers – allows you to look for the partners you need. You may be able to access capital, form strategic alliances, or locate business advice at various stages of your business growth.

Local Investment Networking Company
http://www.linc.co.uk
LINC promotes the National Business Angels Network. This is a nationwide organisation which exists to match private investors – 'business angels' – with entrepreneurs seeking equity funding in the range of £10,000 to £250,000. Its sponsors include Lloyds Bank, the HSBC Bank, NatWest, the Royal Bank of Scotland, Barclays, and the Corporation of London.

Loan Guarantee Scheme
http://www.dti.gov.uk/support/sflgs.htm
If you need help to obtain a bank loan for your business, the long-established loan guarantee scheme run by the Department of Trade & Industry may be the answer. It has helped thousands of small UK businesses over the years.

Start-It
http://www.start-it.co.uk/homepage/index.html
Here you can find out about a venture capital company with a specific interest in the IT and internet sectors and which offers financial, management and accounting support to start-ups.

Fig. 27. The Small Firms Loan Guarantee Scheme has been run for many years by the UK Department of Trade & Industry. It has helped many small firms to get established.

Financial information and services

Bank of England's Euro Page
http://www.bankofengland.co.uk/euro/index.htm
Practical advice for businesses and financiers concerning the intro-duction of the single European currency can be found here.

Checkprint
http://www.checkprint.co.uk/smlbus.htm
Your business stationery is key to the image you project. The design of the cheques you issue could say as much about your business as your letterhead. An APACS accredited cheque printer, working directly with the major banks, Checkprint offers a range of personalised cheque products to suit new and small businesses.

Citizens' Advice Bureau
http://www.nacab.org.uk
The Citizens' Advice Bureau is a good all-round source of information and advice. Your local branch can help you for example with debt problems, and problems with government departments and red tape. This is the address of its national web site. You can also search for the address of your nearest CAB branch.

Financial matters...

Financial Aspects of Freelancing
http://www.brentwoodit.demon.co.uk/financia.htm
You can order this free book which aims to guide the computer freelancer through the financial maze. Its authors are Barry Whiffin and Joanne Berry, partners of BW Whiffin and Co, an accountancy practice with 25 years' experience of handling the taxation affairs of computer freelancers.

Find: The Financial Directory
http://www.find.co.uk/businesses/
This is a well-known internet directories of UK-based financial services – well worth a look. Follow the link to its Business Services Centre.

Moneyweb
http://www.moneyweb.co.uk/cases/selfemp.html
This well-established site enables self-employed people to conduct a financial review, including advice on pensions, permanent health and other forms of insurance, and investments. This page offers some useful starting points.

Online Banking
http://www.onlinebankingreport.com
This is an authoritative and user-friendly source of comment and data on the latest trends in the online banking industry all around the world. It issues a monthly report – the *Online Banking Report* – on home banking together with various interactive financial products. It makes quite a good starting point from which you can explore UK banks and their internet-based services.

Small Business Cash Flow Management Portal
http://www.ctoc.co.uk
The Credit to Cash web site tackles small business and cash flow issues. It aims to provide users with the knowledge and techniques to achieve long-lasting solutions to business problems, and thus to improve their profitability. Designed primarily for UK small businesses, the site contains an extensive business credit management database and offers access to online consumer debt advice.

The Business
http://www.thebusinessuk.com
This site promotes business in the UK and throughout the world, with links into loans, advice, opportunities and information. It provides free links, free offers and various interesting contacts and fraud watch pages, as well as some provocative news and press releases.

Fig. 28. The Business. Take advantage of free offers, interesting links and fraud watch pages through this site.

This Is Money
http://www.thisismoney.com
Another site well worth visiting for general purpose financial information is This Is Money. It contains a special Small Business area containing news and features relevant to the needs of the small business owner. The site is run by Associated New Media, the arm of the Daily Mail & General Trust responsible for online activities.

UK Share Net
http://www.uksharenet.co.uk
The purpose of this site is to gather together links to all the top internet sites relating to UK stocks and shares, investing, company analysis and business news. This site seeks to provide access to all the resources an investor should need.

Insurance

British Insurance Brokers' Association
http://www.biba.org.uk
BIBA is the leading independent UK insurance body, representing both the consumer and the professional insurance broker. Its members operate in the home, motor, travel, commercial and industrial insurance markets, arranging more than three quarters of all such policies in the UK. The web site includes an insurance jargon buster, and the facility to find a broker. There are two ways you can do this – either based on where you live, or based on what risk you want to insure. There are over 350 different types of insurance available, ranging from antiques to musical instruments, from pets to yachts, and covering every type of business insurance.

Financial matters..

Cornhill Insurance
http://www.cornhill.co.uk
Contact your local insurance broker for details of Cornhill's home-business insurance policy – or visit this web site.

Screentrade
http://www.screentrade.co.uk
By visiting this well-known web site, you can compare quotes from leading UK insurance companies and buy motor and household insurance cover online. Screentrade will prepare a number of competitive, personalised quotes for you in a matter of minutes. Then you can compare prices and cover – you may be surprised how policy features differ. Just key in your details once, and you will be in touch with some of the biggest names in the market. When you are ready you can buy online, or over the phone, whichever you prefer.

Tolson Messanger
http://www.tolsonmessenger.co.uk/web/index.htm
Here you can find out about business insurance designed for people working from home.

Worldwide Broker Network (WBN)
http://www.wbnglobal.com
This could be worth a look if you need to arrange insurance overseas. WBN is an integrated worldwide network of independent brokers. It offers a broad range of insurance services, including property, liability, risk management, and employee benefit plans. It has representation in more than 45 countries.

Taxation and regulation

Chartered Institute of Taxation
http://www.tax.org.uk/
This authoritative web site offers tax information and advice for beginners and experts alike. The CIOT is the leading UK professional body concerned solely with taxation. It educates, informs and helps both professionals and the public on matters of tax. Its web site aims to provide comprehensive and current tax information to members, students, tax professionals and those seeking advice.

Companies House
http://www.companies-house.gov.uk
Companies House provides information on how every limited company needs to file its annual accounts, plus an Annual Return, and otherwise comply with company law.

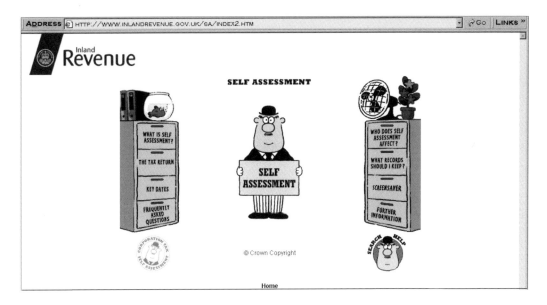

ADDRESS HTTP://WWW.INLANDREVENUE.GOV.UK/SA/INDEX2.HTM

Inland Revenue
http://www.inlandrevenue.gov.uk
Advice on the UK tax system is available straight from the horse's mouth. This site includes various sets of questions and answers for the self-employed and for directors of companies.

Office of Fair Trading
http://www.oft.gov.uk
The OFT site is worth exploring, whether you see yourself as a customer, or as a supplier.

Self Assessment
http://www.inlandrevenue.gov.uk/sa/index2.htm
All you need to know from the Inland Revenue about self assessment, what records to keep, the key dates, frequently asked questions, and more – even a free screensaver can be found here!

Taxtips
http://www.taxtips.co.uk
This is a useful and user-friendly site, providing up to date tax advice for British limited companies and sole traders alike. You can also find tax tables and those all-important deadlines to avoid risking penalties for late payment and filing of returns.

More Internet Handbooks to help you

Personal Finance on the Internet, Graham Jones.
Using Credit Cards on the Internet, Graham Jones.

Fig. 29. Self-assessment for UK income tax. The answers to all your questions should be found in one or other of these drawers.

6 Doing business abroad

In this chapter we will explore:

▶ *how this chapter can help you*
▶ *European resources*
▶ *overseas market information*
▶ *key membership organisations*

. . . .

How this chapter can help you

This chapter describes web sites which can help you:

1. Explore opportunities for doing business in Middle East markets.

2. Link into off-the-shelf research and publications covering the world.

3. Gain access to 500,000 companies across 30 European countries.

4. Find complementary organisations which you can target for links.

5. Develop some new business in Europe.

6. Get help in identifying, selecting and researching the export markets offering the most potential for your products or services.

7. Explore international trade services for manufacturers, importers-exporters, trade service businesses and opportunity seekers.

8. Access advice, training, publications and checklists covering various international trading practices plus analysis and forecasts of the political, economic and business environment in more than 180 countries.

9. Discover new trade opportunities and partners worldwide.

10. Get in touch with chambers of commerce around the world.

European resources

Euromonitor
http://www.euromonitor.com
Euromonitor is a business information publisher. It provides off-the-shelf research and publishes over 200 new titles each year. These

cover the whole world, from the Americas to Asia-Pacific through to Western and Eastern Europe, Africa and the Middle East. The Euromonitor web site offers market statistics as well as a database of reports.

Europages Business Directory
http://www.europages.com
This directory offers details of 500,000 companies across 30 European countries. The site can be viewed in several different languages.

Europages Link Resources
http://www.webpromotion.co.uk/resourcelinks.htm
Use this site to find complementary companies to target for links. There is a nice ability to find online businesses sorted by sector.

European Info Centres
http://www.euro-info.org.uk
Local EICs provide access to a range of specialist information and advisory services to help companies develop their business in Europe. Specialist enquiry services deal with the spectrum of questions which different companies ask about the European business environment. These range from EU and national legislation to technical standards, from R&D programmes to EU funding. In addition, they help businesses with market information through their network contacts and specialist information services. They say: 'By tapping into an up-to-the-minute database, EICs can supply SMEs with a daily, weekly or monthly selection of opportunities relevant to their business.'

Fig. 30. The home page of the European Info Centres network. Take a look at the opportunities, current Euro news and links, and widen your international horizons.

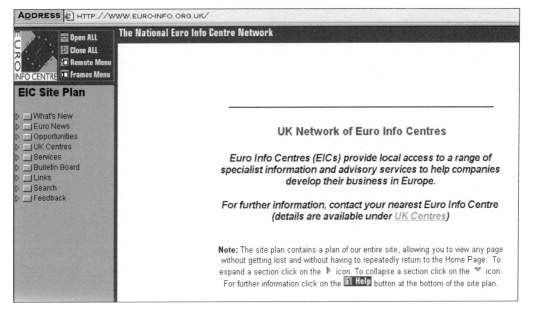

Doing business abroad...

European Investment Bank
http://www.eib.org
The European Investment Bank is the European Union's main financing institution. Its principal task is to contribute towards the integration, balanced development and economic and social cohesion of the member countries. To this end, it raises on the markets substantial volumes of funds that it directs on the most favourable terms towards financing capital projects according with the objectives of the Union. Outside the Union the EIB implements the financial components of agreements concluded under European development aid and co-operation policies.

Treasury – Euro Preparations
http://www.euro.gov.uk
This web site contains information for UK businesses adjusting to the emergence of the Euro.

Overseas market information

British Chambers of Commerce Export Zone
http://www.britishchambers.org.uk/exportzone/
This is a web site for British exporters, specially developed by the British Chambers of Commerce and UPS, the world's largest express delivery company. They say: 'If it's the first time you're thinking about breaking into new markets overseas, or if you're an experienced exporter keen to develop your export operations, this is the site for you. You'll find all the information, advice and links you need to turn your export potential into export success.'

Committee for Middle East Trade
http://www.comet.org.uk
One of the COMET's main objectives is to make British firms aware of the opportunities for doing business in Middle East markets. Its staff has extensive experience of the area and is able to advise on trading conditions in individual markets, sources of information, economic and development trends in the Middle East and general aspects of trade policy.

Economist Intelligence Unit
http://www.eiu.com
The EIU produces objective and timely analysis and forecasts of the political, economic and business environment in more than 180 countries. It also publishes reports on certain strategic industries and the latest management thinking. This is an authoritative and long-established service.

Exporting Expertise Online
http://www.dti.gov.uk/ots/
British Trade International is a global network dedicated to helping UK business compete successfully throughout the world. Its aim is to help UK firms take full advantage of overseas business opportunities by providing support, information, advice and assistance throughout the exporting process.

Export Market Information Centre
http://www.dti.gov.uk/ots/emic/
EMIC is British Trade International's free self-service library for exporters. They can help you identify, select and research the export markets offering the most potential for your products or services.

Global Trade Center
http://ww.wtradezone.com
This site provides many valuable international trade services for manufacturers, importers exporters, trade service businesses and opportunity seekers. See their international trade business opportunities and World Trade Plan, free import export trade leads, famous trade bulletin board, traders web sites and web site advertising services. The site also contains some free sales leads.

Golden Bridge Trade Center
http://www.goldenbridge.ca
You can explore some of the most comprehensive and efficient sources of international trade leads on this site.

HM Customs & Excise
http://www.hmce.gov.uk
The UK Customs & Excise administers or enforces controls on the international movement of goods. These controls are decided by various individual government departments. From the home page follow the link to Information for Business. Here you can check out current information on such topics as rates of exchange for customs purposes and tariff notices.

International Market Research Mall
http://www.imrmall.com
The IMR Mall offers full text market research reports including graphics and charts plus search capabilities.

News
http://www.dti.gov.uk/ots/news/
You can link into overseas trade services through this page maintained by the UK Department of Trade & Industry.

Doing business abroad...

Simpler Trade Procedure Board
http://www.sitpro.org.uk
SITPRO is the UK's national trade facilitation agency. It aims to help business trade more effectively and to simplify the international trading process. It is concerned with the procedures and documentation associated with international trade. SITPRO offers a wide range of services, including advice and training, publications and checklists covering various international trading practices. It manages the UK aligned system of export documents and licences the printers and software suppliers who sell the forms and export document software.

Trade UK Export Database
http://www.tradeuk.com
TradeUK is a free internet service maintained by the British government. Using the latest information technology, it helps international customers search for British suppliers and to deliver their purchasing requirements direct to the desktops of relevant British companies. Through this site you can explore various ecommerce contacts, and identify a range of export sales leads.

Tradeleads Database
http://www.yellowpagesbusiness.co.uk/international.html
This service of Yellow Pages is worth checking out. For example, its Tradeleads Database can help you find an overseas business partner looking to export to the UK.

Yahoo! Countries
http://www.yahoo.co.uk/regional/countries/
Each country section in the massive Yahoo! internet directory includes a very useful section on business and economy. Here you can explore a variety of trade links, business opportunities, economic links, tax information, company listings and much more. This site makes a great starting point for your research.

Key membership organisations

American Chamber of Commerce
http://www.amcham.org.uk
AMCHAM was established in 1916 and for more than 80 years has helped its members to competitively build their international businesses. They are non-profit and reinvest cash flow into programmes for their members.

American Marketing Association
http://www.ama.org
The AMA is America's largest professional society of marketers. It has more than 45,000 members in 92 countries and 500 chapters throughout North America. It provides benefits to marketing profes-

sionals in both business and education and serves all levels of marketing practitioners, educators and students. On its web site you can find out information on the latest trends in marketing strategy, join the Association, or read a sample issue of *Marketing News Online*, its members' journal.

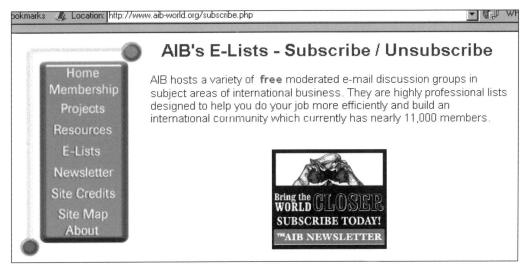

Association for International Business
http://www.aib-world.org
AIB provides a global internet community for its members to share resources, expertise, and problem solving in international business. It provides the members an opportunity to form new strategic alliances and gain a wide prospective on conditions, be they commercial or cultural, in the many countries it serves. AIB has 11,000 members in 200 countries.

British Exporters Association
http://www.bexa.co.uk
BExA is an independent national trade association representing all sectors of the export community. Originally established in 1940 as the National General Export Merchants Group, it became in 1961 the British Export Houses Association. In 1988, with the admission of manufacturers into membership, it assumed its present name. Membership is open to all companies and other organisations resident in the United Kingdom who export goods or services, or who provide assistance to such companies in the promotion and furtherance of export activities.

Institute of Export
http://www.export.org.uk
The Institute of Export is the UK's only national professional awarding body for professional qualifications in international trade and gradu-

Fig. 31. The web site of the Association for International Business. Here you can subscribe to a number of email discussion lists, to exchange business ideas and make new personal contacts.

ate membership of the Institute of Export – MIEx (Grad). The Institute maintains a very useful international trade portal at this address:

http://www.international-trade.org.uk

This provides overseas market information, access to trade finance advice, downloadable international trade education and training material, online travel advice services, assistance with technical and documentation problems and the UK's most comprehensive database of international trade information and tested global links. You can receive its newsletter, *Export News*, free by email to your desktop.

International Chamber of Commerce
http://www.iccwbo.org
This organisation promotes international trade, investment and the market economy system worldwide.

World Chambers of Commerce
http://www.worldchambers.com
This site offers access to a comprehensive directory of chambers of commerce around the world. It contains much of the economic information you need for successful international trading, such as financial reports and customs information. They say: 'Through your local chamber of commerce, your business will find new trade opportunities and partners worldwide. WCN is your key to being a successful business in the 21st century. Its global network of chambers of commerce helps companies of all sizes expand their national and worldwide markets through secured, electronic commerce. Find out how global ecommerce and WCN will help your business grow.'

Fig. 32. World Chambers of Commerce offers a world of business information and contacts at your fingertips.

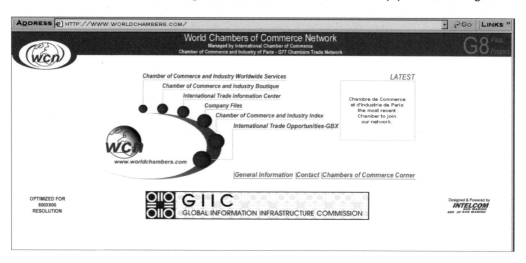

More Internet Handbooks to help you

Marketing a Business on the Internet, Sara Edlington (2nd edition).
Where to Find It on the Internet, Kye Valongo (2nd edition).

7 Business support

In this chapter we will explore:

▶ *how this chapter can help you*
▶ *business discussion and news*
▶ *business names*
▶ *business networks*
▶ *business supplies*
▶ *businesses for sale and wanted*
▶ *government departments*
▶ *newsletters and magazines*
▶ *other business support*

. . . .

How this chapter can help you

This chapter describes web sites which can help you:

1. Access the latest news for the small and home business.

2. Get in touch with local chambers of commerce.

3. Find out about certification and standards.

4. Source the business assets and IT equipment you need.

5. Find small business information on taxation and law, marketing and manpower.

6. Take part in online business discussion.

7. View businesses for sale by owners and agents.

8. Find out about the requirements of the Data Protection Act.

9. Explore government support and fact sheets for small businesses.

10. Find valuable information and links designed for the 'netrepreneur'.

11. Investigate telecommuting, teleworking, the virtual office and related topics.

12. Access business start-up help, including finding a mentor or business adviser.

13. Check out planning permission for using your home for work.

14. Benefit from a variety of business manuals and fact sheets.

15. Get free tips and advice for building your sales, profits and cash flow.

Business discussion and news

Business Discussion Forums
http://tile.net/lists/learningfount.html
Here you can link into a discussion list on business strategy from Learning Fount and an email discussion list on business strategy. Learning Fount is a vehicle for building a community of entrepreneurs and executives by exchanging ideas and experiences related to the development and use of good business strategies.

Business Newsgroups
http://www.deja.com
Deja offers web-based access to tens of thousands of Usenet newsgroups. The following newsgroups and newsgroup categories may be of interest:

uk.business	aol.commerce.mim.announce
fr.business	alt.business.franchise
alt.business	alt.business.import-export
misc.entrepreneurs	alt.business.import-export.services
biz.marketplace	uk.business.telework

If you have never accessed newsgroups before, a quick way of doing so is to type any of the above names into the address panel of your browser, prefixed with 'news:' (without quote marks). For example:

news:uk.business.telework

Cobweb Information & News
http://www.cobwebinfo.com
Cobweb Information is an organisation whose resolution is to discover and publish original business knowledge. Cobweb strives to provide a complete service that will fulfil the fundamental needs of businesses and their intermediaries by delivering relevant knowledge that is instructive, informative and revealing.

Discussion Boards
http://www.bizweb2000.com/wwwboard/
http://homebusiness-websites.com/cgi-bin/index.cgi
http://talk.businessbug.com/
http://www.profitalk.com/

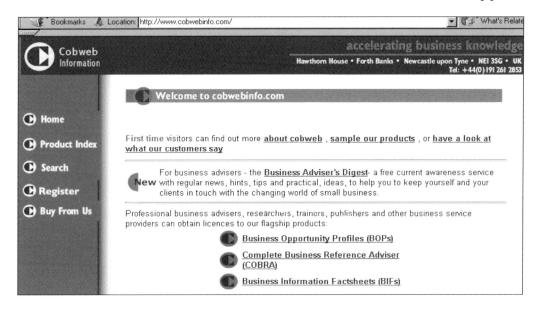

Cobweb
Information

accelerating business knowledge
Hawthorn House • Forth Banks • Newcastle upon Tyne • NEI 3SG • UK
Tel: +44(0) 191 261 2853

Welcome to cobwebinfo.com

- Home
- Product Index
- Search
- Register
- Buy From Us

First time visitors can find out more **about cobweb** , **sample our products** , or **have a look at what our customers say**

New For business advisers - the **Business Adviser's Digest**- a free current awareness service with regular news, hints, tips and practical, ideas, to help you to keep yourself and your clients in touch with the changing world of small business.

Professional business advisers, researchers, trainers, publishers and other business service providers can obtain licences to our flagship products:

- **Business Opportunity Profiles (BOPs)**
- **Complete Business Reference Adviser (COBRA)**
- **Business Information Factsheets (BIFs)**

Business names

Business Names Register
http://www.bnr.plc.uk
For a small fee, the Business Names Register will search over 3,000,000 business names and 600,000 registered trademarks to ensure your name does not conflict with anyone else's. It will also help you protect your own business's name.

Business networks

British Chambers of Commerce
http://www.britishchambers.org.uk/
The BCC is the 'national voice' of Britain's 60 chambers of commerce, representing 110,000 businesses. Information about local chambers and features on issues that affect British firms, such as the Euro, minimum wage and working time directive can be found here.

Business Networks 2000
http://www.businessnetworks2000.com/front.htm
This site offers business-to-business networking opportunities, information, advice and related events.

Federation of Small Businesses
http://www.fsb.org.uk
The FSB is a non-political organisation aimed at helping small businesses. It also provides members with various benefits including: a legal advice line covering English and Scottish law, as well as tax, VAT and health and safety issues; a special insurance policy which gives

Fig. 33. Cobweb is a useful UK-based resource for people running their own businesses.

cover for legal and professional fees, criminal prosecutions, employment disputes, jury service among other things; and a regular magazine for members. Regional branches hold regular meetings for members.

First Tuesday
http://www.firsttuesday.com/
A collection of resources can be found here for the internet entrepreneur with an eye on Europe. The enterprise runs a series of meeting places for people, money and ideas in new media.

Franchise Business
http://www.franchisebusiness.co.uk/
This organisation offers a focal point for UK franchising.

Institute of Business Advisors
http://www.iba.org.uk/
The Institute of Business Advisors can help you find a mentor or business adviser. It also offers a range of publications covering all aspects of starting and running your own business.

Business supplies

Business Auctions.com
http://www.business-auctions.com/
Access a site that sells business-to-business assets and IT equipment.

DIY Contracts
http://www.cracker.u-net.com
Instant Contracts (module one) has been developed by CCA Software to generate standard legal contracts of employment. The software allows you to draw up or change a contract of employment, and generate employee non-competition agreements, non-disclosure agreements and even partnership agreements. CCA Software has also developed Instant Contracts (module two), which contains all the legal paperwork necessary to get rid of troublesome employees, from the first official warning letter to the final termination notice.

Office Shopper
http://www.officeshopper.com
An ecommerce solution for your office needs can be found here.

Office World Direct
http://www.office-world.co.uk
Visit an online superstore where you can choose from over 5,000 products. These range from office supplies and stationery to furniture and business products, plus information about the chain's 59 'real-world' stores.

Online Business Cards
http://www.online-business-cards.astra.co.uk/
Visit this site to advertise your own business and to view the sites of other businesses.

Practical Guide to Business Contracts
http://www.bnetp.co.uk/
This site offers a basic introduction to business agreements and contract law written by a lawyer for the businessman who wants a basic, common sense framework to assist preliminary contract discussions (published by Business Network Publishing).

Viking Direct
http://www.vikingdirect.com
You can find a vast range of items for offices, shops and warehouses through this site. Ask for 'the cheapest price' since prices vary between their regular catalogues. Tip: never quote the code that identifies the catalogue unless it starts with a Y (one of Viking's cheapest catalogues).

Businesses for sale and wanted

Business Sales
http://www.businesssales.com
Through this site, you can find out about businesses for sale by owners and agents. You can search through 12,000 businesses for sale in the United States, UK, South Africa, Australia and 70 other countries.

Government departments

Business Link
http://www.businesslink.co.uk
Business Link is the umbrella site for the UK government's small business support network.

Fig. 34. Business Link. For impartial advice and business support, look for your local business link through this home page.

Business support...

Business Matters
http://www.business.knowledge.com
The Starting Up section contains information relevant when you are first setting up a new business presented as a step-by-step guide. The Day-to-Day section is more general and contains information that is not necessarily part of setting up a business, but which is nevertheless useful for its day to day running. This section is sub-divided into subject areas. The Features section offers guest articles, and a forum where you can air your views.

Companies Registration Office
http://www.companieshouse.gov.uk
Companies House has two main functions: the incorporation, re-registration and striking off of companies and the registration of documents required to be filed under companies, insolvency and related legislation and the provision of company information to the public, for which purpose they enforce compliance with statutory requirements.

Department of Trade and Industry
http://www.dti.gov.uk
The site includes abundant information about government support for business, including the New Deal and the Small Firms Loan Guarantee Scheme.

DTI Regulatory Guides: Employment
http://www.dti.gov.uk/IR/regs.htm
Here you can find essential official fact sheets on everything from disability discrimination to itemised pay statements.

Data Protection
http://www.dataprotection.gov.uk/guide.htm
Here you can study a 40-page guide issued by the Data Protection Registrar. This gives advice on how the Data Protection Act 1984 affects homeworkers. The Guide is aimed at clubs, associations, charities, people who are running their own business or employees who work at home, either occasionally or regularly. Since almost all businesses that keep records on clients need to be registered, it is important that they are correctly registered. This has been made easier with the assisted pre-filling of forms available on the Registration Line: (01625) 545740. Copies of the booklet or more information about the Act are available from the Information Line: (01625) 545745.

Health & Safety Executive
http://www.open.gov.uk/hse/hsehome.htm
Here you will find a site providing information about legal health and safety requirements, many of which apply to small businesses.

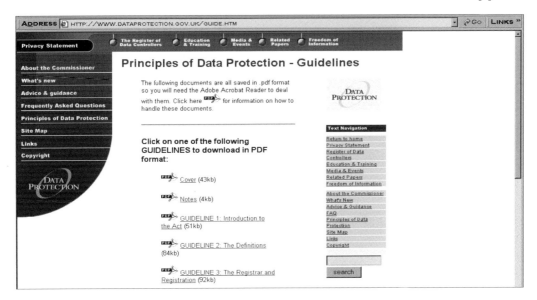

ADDRESS HTTP://WWW.DATAPROTECTION.GOV.UK/GUIDE.HTM   Go   LINKS »

Privacy Statement   The Register of Data Controllers   Education & Training   Media & Events   Related Papers   Freedom of Information

About the Commissioner

What's new

Advice & guidance

Frequently Asked Questions

Principles of Data Protection

Site Map

Links

Copyright

DATA PROTECTION

Principles of Data Protection - Guidelines

The following documents are all saved in .pdf format so you will need the Adobe Acrobat Reader to deal with them. Click here for information on how to handle these documents.

DATA PROTECTION

Click on one of the following GUIDELINES to download in PDF format:

Cover (43kb)

Notes (4kb)

GUIDELINE 1: Introduction to the Act (51kb)

GUIDELINE 2: The Definitions (84kb)

GUIDELINE 3: The Registrar and Registration (92kb)

Text Navigation

Return to home
Privacy Statement
Register of Data Controllers
Education & Training
Media & Events
Related Papers
Freedom of Information

About the Commissioner
What's New
Advice & Guidance
FAQ
Principles of Data Protection
Site Map
Links
Copyright

search

Information Society Initiative
http://www.isi.gov.uk/isi/
The DTI's Information Society Initiative offers small businesses some impartial advice on using information and communications technologies.

Patent Office
http://www.patent.gov.uk/snews/index.html
You can check out information about how to legally protect your creative ideas through this site.

Planning Permission
http://www.homeworking.co.uk/library/planper.htm
Find out about planning permission and what it means for using your home as your place of business.

Small Business Advice Service
http://www.smallbusinessadvice.org.uk
This is a service maintained by the National Federation of Enterprise Agencies. It provides free business advice and guidance to anyone planning or starting-up a new business, or running an established small business with fewer than 10 employees, in England. It offers access to a growing range of business information and tools including reference documents, checklists, business planning software, links to other external information sources and services – all aimed at supporting you and your new business. A unique feature of this service is its business enquiry service, which can link you directly to one of 200 or more accredited business advisers located throughout England. The enquiry service operates by email.

Fig. 35. Don't get caught out by the new UK Data Protection laws. Visit this site to find out how to cover yourself and stay on the right side of the law.

Business support..

Trading Standards
http://www.tradingstandards.gov.uk
This is your one stop shop for consumer protection information in the UK. The site is supported and maintained by ITSA, the Institute of Trading Standards Administration. This site provides a wealth of information for consumers and businesses, schools, advice and information centres, community organisations, local councils, business support agencies and trade associations.

Newsletters and magazines

At Home Professionals E-Zine
http://www.homeprofessionals.com
This is a resource for professionals who already work at home and those who would like to start.

Best Biz Ideas
http://tile.net/lists/bestbizideas.html
A free monthly newsletter for small and home business owners can be accessed through this home page. It includes lots of ideas for starting and running a small or home business, including new business ideas, marketing and sales ideas, hot links and tips. The newsletter does not publish MLM, network marketing or 'business opportunity' promotions.

Better Business Online
http://www.better-business.co.uk
Better Business is the UK's leading small business subscription magazine. It says it will help you succeed in your business whether you are a one-man band working from home or a growing enterprise. On this site you will find a whole range of useful stuff including the latest news for small businesses, contacts and links, free fact sheets, plus proven profit boosters together with bargain offers and book reviews.

Business Zone – SME News
http://www.businesszone.co.uk
Business Zone describes itself as 'the everyday resource for UK business professionals on the internet'. It covers news, links, databases, a directory, a press zone and tax facts.

Online User
http://www.onlineinc.com
You can read the full text of this practical magazine aimed at people who use online resources for business and professional reasons.

Practical Cash Online Magazine
http://www.ipw.com/pc/
This lively online publication offers a wealth of ideas for effective advertising, networking and marketing.

Other business support

Bird-Online
http://www.bird-online.co.uk
Bird-Online is accredited by the DTI and Business Link supported Enterprise Zone and is an information and communication resource for business in the UK and Ireland. It is widely used by small businesses, researchers, consultants, business support agencies, and blue chip corporations. The site offers quick and easy access to detailed information on business areas you need to know about, in a format that is straightforward. It is a meeting place for businesses, where you can make contact regarding business opportunities, find a consultant for your business needs, and use free and confidential checklists on a number of key business topics such as marketing and human resources management.

BizzAdvice
http://www.bizzadvice.com
BizzAdvice describes itself as a pan-European information marketplace for starting-up or growing a business. They say: 'We connect people in need of information and advice with people who have the knowledge and background to help others become successful. Our pan-European vision allows you to ask experts in any given country about local tax issues, local legislations, business policies etc.'

BSI
http://www.bsi.org.uk
Formerly the British Standards Institution, the BSAI handles certification and standards. Its web site features a searchable database.

Business Bureau
http://www.businessbureau-uk.co.uk
Information for small businesses, from taxation to the law, marketing to manpower, general accountancy and business travel can be found here – plus a beginner's guide to the internet.

CAROL
http://www.carol.co.uk
This is a free service offering one-point access to British and European company annual reports online.

Business support..

Enterprise Zone
http://www.enterprisezone.org.uk
The Enterprise Zone can help you with links to information, resources, or sources of expertise on finance, IT, marketing, HR, export and other key business issues. The Enterprise Zone is a gateway to business information for SMEs.

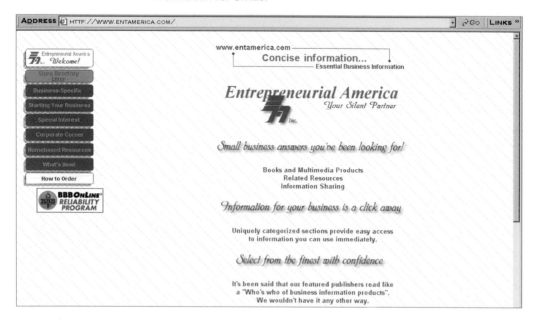

Fig. 36. Entrepreneurial America Inc. Click onto the homebased resources for starters.

Entrepreneurial America
http://www.entamerica.com
This is a site offering books, multimedia products, home-based re-sources and information sharing for starting your business.

Entrepreneurs Corner
http://www.makestuff.com/home_business/index.html
This could be a good place to brainstorm for ideas relating to writing, photography, arts and crafts.

Entrepreneurs Guide
http://www.entrepreneurs.about.com
Information and links for the entrepreneur can be found on this site, which is part of the sprawling and ever-expanding About.com net-work. An enormous range of topics is covered.

Gil Gorden Associates
http://www.gilgordon.com
This site consolidates a wide variety of information from around the world on telecommuting, teleworking, the virtual office, and related topics.

Go Contract!
http://www.gocontract.com
This site helps would-be computer consultants set up in business.

Kogan Page Publishers
http://www.kogan-page.co.uk
Kogan Page is perhaps the best-known independent UK publisher of practical books and other materials for small business management. From its home page you can link into a variety of resources for career development, training and business management.

Mail Order Protection Scheme
http://www.mops.org.uk
MOPS acts as a guarantor for newspaper advertisers. It protects consumers who purchase by mail order if an advertiser covered by the scheme goes bust. MOPS only covers cash-off-the-page advertising in national daily newspapers. Ads carry the little MOPS logo.

NatWest Small Business Planner

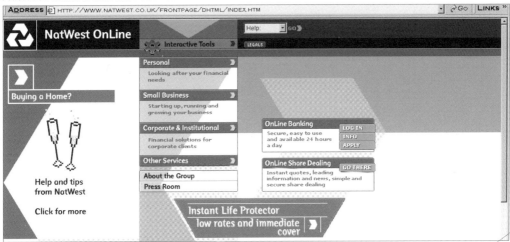

http://www.natwest.co.uk
To download the free planner software, select from the top dropdown menu 'small business' then follow the links to 'starting a business' then 'setting up a business'.

Fig. 37. Natwest's Small Business Planner. Through this home page you can find out how to plan a sucessful business step-by-step.

Net Institute
http://www.netinstitute.com
This site offers help to home-based business who want to make money on the internet.

Power Freelancing
http://home.earthlink.net/~georgesoren/index.htm
Tips for the freelancer plus a bookstore to visit can be found here.

Business support..

Self Employment Business Manuals
http://www.atlantica.co.uk/business/dsclarke.html
Through this site, you can access self-employment business manuals that provide information to locate and benefit from homework or self-employment. Find out the secrets of super success in mail order and low cost home businesses.

Shell LiveWire
http://www.shell-livewire.org
The famous oil company offers some sound advice to budding entrepreneurs (16-30) about setting up and developing their own businesses. This great looking site has information about their Young Entrepreneur of the Year award scheme and a discussion forum.

Small Business Research Portal
http://www.smallbusinessportal.co.uk

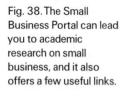
Fig. 38. The Small Business Portal can lead you to academic research on small business, and it also offers a few useful links.

This portal has been designed to provide links to internet sites that will be helpful to fellow small business researchers. There are links to books, centres, conferences, government agencies, institutes, a jobs archive, mega-sites, message boards, news, publications, a quotes archive, research tools and reviews.

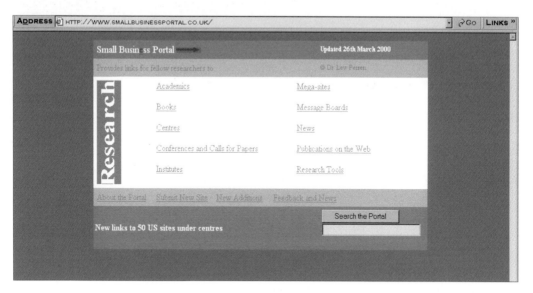

Smart Eric
http://www.smarteric.com
Support, advice and resources for freelancers and the self-employed are available through this breezy home page. Freelancers can register to receive Smart Eric's regular email newsletter. Features of the site include links and resources to get you started and help you succeed, and 'networking for success' where they say you can meet new

people to bring in new business and consolidate your position in the marketplace.

Start Business
http://www.startbusiness.co.uk
This award-winning site aims to help all those new to, or considering, self-employment. They say they will endeavour to give a response to your start-up questions within 24 hours. Either an experienced business adviser, or someone who is self-employed will deal with your questions, in confidence. You can click onto links for marketing, finance, grants, resources, tips and books.

The Biz
http://www.thebiz.co.uk
The well-known Biz Directory aims to be a comprehensive listing of business-to-business resources across the UK, whether they have an online presence or not.

UK Trade Fairs & Exhibitions
http://www.exhibitions.co.uk
This is the leading web site for the UK exhibition industry. It is sponsored by British Trade International, the new UK government organisation responsible for all official trade promotion and development work. The site offers a comprehensive listing of all forthcoming consumer, public, industrial and trade exhibitions held in major venues around the UK. You can search the list by exhibition type, by exhibition date, by exhibition organiser, or by exhibition venue. The data is updated regularly at the beginning of each month.

Virtual Office Survival Handbook
http://www.tjobs.com/virtofc.htm
Here you can find the telecommuter and the entrepreneur's practical manual to starting, managing and thriving in a virtual office by Alice Bredin and published by John Wiley & Sons. It contains advice on working in all types of virtual offices, including the home office, satellite work centre, time-shared workspace and mobile office.

World of Work
http://www.telework.org.uk
If you want to find out more about teleworking, working for yourself or working in a small business, visit this web site. It has been designed and created to act as a portal for content that is related to the world of work – employment, self-employment, full or part time economic activity of individuals. It aims to provide a range of links, resources and information that will help people who work, in whatever capacity that might be, including voluntary work undertaken for the community or charities.

Business support ....

Yahoo! Small Business

Featured Sponsors	**Your Business**

PIP PRINTING

YAHOO! Store
Start something big.

Small Business Resource Center

- **Start Your Business**
  Guide to getting you started in a new business.
- **Put your Business Online**
  Ready for the world to see your business online.
- **Manage your Business**
  Widen your customer base.

Take our Small Business Survey

Topics

Communications	Ecommerce
Finance	Government Services
Human Resources	International Bus./Trade
Legal	Office Supplies
Printing	Sales and Marketing
Startup Basics	Technology

Solutions
- Get a Web Site
- Sell Online
- Promote Your Business
- Business Essentials

Featured Articles

Fig. 39. Yahoo!'s small business portal site contains links to lots of advice to get you started.

Yahoo! Small Business
http://smallbusiness.yahoo.com
Tips and advice for building your clientele can be found through this essential portal.

8 Ecommerce

In this chapter we will explore:

▶ *how this chapter can help you*
▶ *associations*
▶ *awards*
▶ *business discussion*
▶ *export*
▶ *general ecommerce resources*
▶ *payment systems*
▶ *press releases and media*
▶ *research and reports*
▶ *shop building software*
▶ *taxation of ecommerce*
▶ *web developers*

. . . .

How this chapter can help you

This chapter introduces web sites which can help you:

1. Access advice for small businesses planning to use the internet.

2. Submit articles and press releases to ezines.

3. Reach into global markets by using the internet.

4. Get in touch with web designers specialising in ecommerce.

5. Find out about hit counters and visitor tracking systems.

6. Set up a merchant account for your online business.

7. Explore good business practice in an ecommerce environment.

8. Subscribe to free ezines and newsletters which cover your area of interest.

9. Examine taxation issues in electronic commerce.

10. Get a free legal overview of your web site.

11. Learn about secure online buying and selling.

12. Explore shop-building software and other web site development services.

Associations

CommerceNet
http://www.commerce.net
CommerceNet is a non-profit membership organisation which aims to meet the evolving needs of companies doing electronic commerce. Since its founding in 1994, its mission has been to promote and advance 'interoperable electronic commerce' to support emerging communities of commerce. This community of influential ecommerce decision-makers is over 600 strong, with a focus on business-to-business ecommerce worldwide. The web site contains such resources as research reports, advocacy & public policy resources, internet demographics and ecommerce statistics.

eCentre UK
http://www.e-centre.org.uk
eCentreUK is the trading name of the Association for Standards and Practices in ElectronicTrade. It was launched in 1998 with the merger of the Article Number Association and the Electronic Commerce Association. The combined organisation has over 15,000 members. Over 90 per cent are users and over 90 per cent are small and medium enterprises (SMEs). The membership reflects most trade and industry sectors, and is representative of both users and suppliers. The Association offers a one stop shop for help and advice on electronic commerce to UK organisations at large, and provides a comprehensive suite of services to its members to help them to adopt best practice in doing business electronically.

Awards

Ecommerce Awards Scheme
http://www.isi-interforum-awards.com
These awards celebrate and reward UK small and medium sized companies (SMEs) which have been successful in doing business electronically. Regional competitors can each win £5,000, and the national winner wins £30,000. The web site includes an application guide. The judges take into account: (1) integration of electronic commerce into normal business, (2) innovative use of information and communication technology business, (3) benefits obtained in terms of competitive advantage, increased turnover, profit, market penetration or entry into new markets, and (4) future plans based on current experience of electronic commerce. See also:

http://www.ecommerce-awards.co.uk

Virtual Promote Awards
http://www.virtualpromote.com/hotsites.html
This site offers some convenient links to some of the most important

ADDRESS HTTP://WWW.ISHNTERFORUM-AWARDS.COM/   Go   LINKS »

Please follow the link above to the ISI/InterForum ecommerce awards 2000 website.

The ISI/*Inter*Forum **E-Commerce Awards**

a p p l i c a t i o n   g u i d e

award sites on the internet, and masses of extra information about entries and winners.

Fig. 40. The E-Commerce Awards Scheme. Is your web site good enough to win an award? This is the place to find out.

Business discussion

Adam J Boettiger's I-Advertising Digest
http://www.internetadvertising.org
Here you can link into a moderated global discussion group concerned with internet advertising, marketing and online commerce.

Export

AWE
http://www.actonwebexport.com
AWE enables businesses to expand into global markets through the internet and also provides guidance on language and web site translation and using a web site to market and sell to Europe.

General ecommerce resources

Business 2.0
http://www.business2.com
This is an ecommerce business directory aimed at the hi-tech executive. Categories include advertising, finance, general news, and market research.

CyberCount
http://www.cybercount.com/
The site contains details of a free hit-counter and visitor tracking system for web masters.

Ecommerce ....

Home   Careers   The Team   About Us   How To Find Us   Feedback   Links

① Contents   ② Services   ③ What's New   ④ Survey

K▲LT●NS
SOLICITORS

Kaltons... the Property & Internet Lawyers

Kaltons is a niche law practice specialising in e-commerce and property, truly a "clicks & mortar" firm. We believe you will find us refreshingly different and ready to help you face the exciting opportunities of the Third Millennium.

Kaltons have one of the country's leading e-commerce teams and represent some of the Internet's most exciting e-entrepreneurs. Our clients range from modest "e-start-ups" to government departments and a $20bn IT company. We are also proud to be the lawyers to the British Web Design & Marketing Association.

TheRegister   Pirates named and shamed on Web

Fig. 41. Kaltons is a City of London firm of solicitors that specialises in ecommerce. The partnership offers professional help for all firms including the fledgling entrepreneur.

Kaltons
http://www.kaltons.co.uk
This is the web site of the internet lawyers' ecommerce team. To obtain a free appraisal of your own web site, take a look at their online web site risk assessment questionnaire.

Marketing Resource Center
http://www.marketingsource.com/
The Marketing Resource Center is designed to assist businesses with both their traditional and internet marketing efforts.

Sell It on the Web
http://sellitontheweb.com/
You can link here into news, a message board, web store reviews, and step-by-step guides with some useful tips on starting an internet-based business.

Trade to Trade
http://www.tradetotrade.co.uk/
Trade to Trade is a service for manufacturers, wholesalers, importers, distributors and retailers worldwide to source and sell to each other.

Web Promotion
http://www.webpromotion.co.uk/
Free resources for web professionals and online businesses can be viewed on this site with hundreds of links, articles, tools, news and views on web site promotion.

Payment systems

Datacash
http://www.datacash.com/
Datacash can quickly set up a merchant account for you enabling you to take transactions from most major credit cards, including Visa, MasterCard, American Express and debit cards: Switch, Solo and Delta.

Ecash Internet Payment System
http://www.ecashtechnologies.com
eCashTechnologies develops, markets, and supports the eCash software suite, a solution for secure, private, and non-repudiable (nonfraudulent) electronic cash transactions on the internet.

MasterCard International & Electronic Commerce
http://www.mastercard.com/shoponline/set/
This site offers reassuring information about secure online buying with Mastercard's Secure ElectronicTransactions (SET) technology.

SecuraPAY
http://www.securapay.co.uk/
This site offers secure payment systems for e-business applications to help you benefit from the vast market potential the internet offers.

VISA Payment Guidelines
http://www.visa.com

Press releases and media

Article Submission
http://www.web-source.net/articlesub.htm
http://www.ideamarketers.com/
You can automate the submission of articles to ezines through both these sites.

Ecommerce Weekly
http://www.eweekly.com/
Formerly published as *Entrepreneur Weekly*, this is a free weekly newsletter designed to bring you the latest online sales, marketing, and ecommerce strategies to help you succeed in the online environment. In addition, it publishes the latest news of companies and services geared to helping internet entrepreneurs develop their businesses on the net.

e-first
http://www.e-first.co.uk
Explore this monthly ecommerce magazine for business managers.

Fig. 42. E-Zine search is a good place to track down internet magazines covering a vast range of different topics.

Ezines
http://ezinesearch.com
http://list-resources.com
You can use these two sites to search for ezines and newsletters covering your own particular area of interest. Email the editors and ask them if they accept article submissions.

Net Profit
http://www.net-profit.co.uk
This monthly newsletter, published in London, reports on how businesses can get the most out of the internet. You can get it in print or by email by subscribing online.

Press Release Services
http://www.PRweb.com
http://www.webaware.co.uk/netset/text
You can submit your own press releases through these free press release services.

Web Marketing Today
http://www.wilsonweb.com/wmt/
Here you can link into a free twice-monthly electronic newsletter about internet marketing and doing business on the web.

Business research and reports

Communications and Information Industries division of the DTI
http://www.dti.gov.uk/future-unit/
Here you can explore various UK government projects such as the

Information Society Initiative, IT for ALL, UK liaison with the EU's Framework RTD programme, e-commerce, information security, and more.

Converging Technology: Consequences for the Knowledge-Driven Economy
http://www.dti.gov.uk/future-unit/complete/converging/
The site contains details of the 1998 report produced by the Future Unit of the UK Department for Trade & Industry. You can download this document as an Adobe Acrobat PDF file.

e-commerce@its.best.uk
http://www.cabinet-office.gov.uk/innovation/1999/ecommerce/index.htm
Here you can explore a report from the Cabinet Office Performance and Innovation Unit, issued in September 1999. It stated three key priorities – to overcome business inertia; to ensure that government's own actions drive the take-up of ecommerce; and to ensure better co-ordination between government and industry to gain maximum benefit from existing and proposed programmes. A number of other government reports are available, and can be downloaded as PDF files.

Electronic Communications Bill
http://www.parliament.the-stationery-office.co.uk/pa/cm199900/cmbills/004/2000004.htm
The Bill, sponsored by the Department of Trade & Industry, was aimed at fast track facilitation of electronic commerce (November 1999).

Electronic Commerce Agenda for the UK
http://www.dti.gov.uk/cii/ecom.htm
This is a government statement on electronic commerce, published in October 1998.

Forrester
http://www.forrester.com
A leading independent internet research organisation, Forrester has produced some interesting analysis of, and comments about, electronic shopping in Europe, where it surveyed 17,000 households. Online shopping is still very new, and attitudes of consumers and retailers still being formed. But generally, it expects that a much higher proportion of Europeans will adopt a digital lifestyle in the next few years.

InterForum UK Advisory Organisation
http://www.interforum.org
InterForum's activities are meant to raise awareness of the many business opportunities and challenges presented by new information and communications technologies such as the internet. InterForum seeks

etsite: http://www.forrester.com/Home/0,3257,1,FF.html ▼ 🗐 What's Related

FORRESTER

> FORRESTER EUROPE

HELPING BUSINESS THRIVE ON TECHNOLOGY CHANGE

▶ The Forrester Difference

▶ Research & Analysis

A complete portfolio
for your eBusiness Voyage™

BROWSE OUR RESEARCH BY:

Coverage Areas ▼

See How Forrester Can Help You
◉ View Video

Strategy Research

Technographics® Data

Assessment Tools

Events

Advisory Services

FORRESTER MAKES THE CALL

Holiday 2000 Brought Cheer To Online Retail - December 27

3Com Wins With Newfound Foc - December 22

Firms Should Ignore Keynote's Transaction Ratings - December 2

George F. Colony's My View: X Internet

▶ Retail Index

NRF/Forrester
Online Retail Index

▶ In Focus

Holiday Shopping's
Online Buzz

▶ eBusiness Assessment Tools

NEW!
eBusiness TechRankings

Fig. 43. Forrester is one of the better-known and more authoritative sources of research into the latest internet and ecommerce trends.

to ensure that education, legislation, and technology are developed to help British businesses profit from the digital economy.

Internet User Statistics
http://www.net-profit.co.uk
Net Profit is a leading European source of information and analysis on the commercial uses of the internet and other interactive media. It is a London-based research and publishing company with a base of in-house knowledge on electronic commerce.

Jupiter Communications
http://www.jup.com
Jupiter Communications is an established provider of research on internet commerce. Its research, which is solely focused on the inter-net economy, provides clients with comprehensive views of industry trends, forecasts and best practices. The company's research services are provided through continuous subscription. Jupiter Communications is based in New York City, with operations in London, San Francisco, Stockholm, Sydney and Tokyo.

Office of the e-Envoy
http://www.e-envoy.gov.uk/
The Prime Minister has said he is committed to making the UK the best place in the world for ecommerce. The job of the e-Envoy is to coordinate the government's drive towards this ambitious goal.

Reference to EU Legislation in the Field of Information Society
http://www.ispo.cec.be/infosoc/legreg.html
The EU's Information Society Project Office (ISPO) provides links to
many EU and EC documents.

Select Committee on Trade and Industry Tenth Report: Electronic
Commerce
http://www.parliament.the-stationery-office.co.uk/pa/cm199899/
cmselect/cmtrdind/648/64804.htm
This is a report from July 1999, which was based on a wide-ranging
inquiry into electronic commerce. It focused on those aspects of
policy within DTI's remit, but also considered broader issues of rele-
vance to UK consumers and firms.

Shop building software

The following ecommerce software packages have all been favour-
ably reviewed by the internet press and all retailed at less than £600 at
the time of this book being written:

123uk.net
http://www.123uk.net/
Internet business services, including web hosting, dial-up, site
design, secure online trading, promotions and advertising are on
offer from this UK company.

Actinic
http://www.actinic.co.uk
Actinic is one of the better known UK suppliers of software for internet retailing. This is a good place to find some realistic and practical

Fig. 44. The web site of
the UK software
producer Actinic. The
company produces
Actinic Catalog, retail
software specially
designed to enable small
and medium-sized
companies to set up
their own internet sales
channel.

advice for small businesses wishing to use the internet, including information on internet commerce. The site includes details of Actinic's own electronic retailing products, credit card processing, free evaluation, FAQs, customer testimonials and a guide to ecommerce for the small and medium sized enterprise. There are links to a number of live retail web sites which are based on Actinic's products.

Builder Pro

http://www.multiactive.co.uk

This software uses wizards to step you through the template-based store-building process, plus support for all international currencies. The site also offers Shopmaster that supports 10 different currencies with 5 discount rates and checks email addresses to avoid fraud. They say: 'Whether they contact you on the web, via email, by phone or fax, or in person, your customers receive a personalised, one to one experience. You know who they are and what they want – automatically. Good customer service means more loyal customers – and a better return on your investment.'

E-catalist

http://www.e-catalist.com

This Suffolk-based company offers a reasonably straightforward-looking approach to an ecommerce site. They say: 'We develop your customised template to automatically show products, categories and special offers.' E-catalist is a scalable online catalogue solution which can be tailored to your specific needs. It can support secure credit card transactions, be linked into your back office if needed and be operated easily and quickly with your own personalised interface. Templates let you hit the ground running. You just add your own custom text and graphics to the templates, and your web pages are ready to go.

EROL

http://www.erol.co.uk

They say: 'Build the most beautiful online store of your life.' EROL stands for Electronic Retail Online. The firm produces software which works entirely off-line, offering its users complete control over design, a shopping basket, easy store maintenance and editing facilities, and the ability to handle an unlimited number of products. Small Store 2.1 – an updated version of EROL Small Store Edition – was distributed free on the cover of the UK magazine *Internet Works* in January 2001.

SetUpShop.co.uk

http://www.setupshop.co.uk/

This is an easy-to-follow guide to UK ecommerce and ebusiness. The site aims to provide everything you need to know to open a branch of your British shop or business on the web. It includes a discussion forum, so that you can tell them what you have discovered, or ask your peers for help. It also summarises some of the differences between US and UK web shopping.

Shop@ssistant
http://www.floyd.co.uk
Run by the Floyd Consultancy Ltd, this software package offers ready-made pages that can be customised, a site that can be managed off-line, and the ability to calculate an unlimited number of tax rates. Shops can be viewed on all version 3 browsers or later versions.

Taxation of ecommerce

Inland Revenue
http://www.nds.coi.gov.uk
Here you can read an Inland Revenue and Customs & Excise joint paper on UK policy on taxation issues created as a result of electronic commerce.

Web developers

Chameleon Net
http://www.chameleonnet.co.uk/
Based in Harrow, Middlesex, Chameleon are web designers specialising in ecommerce sites. Here they outline their services including shopping carts, multi-lingual and multi-currency support. Their expertise includes database driven websites, customer profiling, secure transaction processing, 24 hour support, online auctions, complex search facilities, and order management.

Ecommerce Solutions
http://www.webfusion.co.uk
WebFusion Internet Solutions is one of the UK's larger web hosting providers, hosting in excess of 15,000 virtual servers and thousands more domain names. They have the technical ability and business management to host and manage your web site.

Ethos
http://www.ethos-design.com
Ethos is a web design and marketing firm based in North Yorkshire. Its web site includes a digital media section and another section for firms wanting to do online selling. Its 'eTailer' suite offers a range of products to enable retailers to succeed online.

iCat
http://www.icat.com
iCat is a division of Intel Online Services, a leading provider of ecommerce software and services to small and medium-sized businesses.

Set Up Shop
What are the things you need to think about when putting your shop on the web?

UK, OK?
We summarise the difference between US and UK web shopping.

Off Your Trolley
We look at the different ways of running a shop, and give links to some of the catalogue packages designed for British business.

Payment
Taking money is what it is all comes down to in the end! We look at the choices you have in the UK, and provide links to some providers.

Ecommerce ....

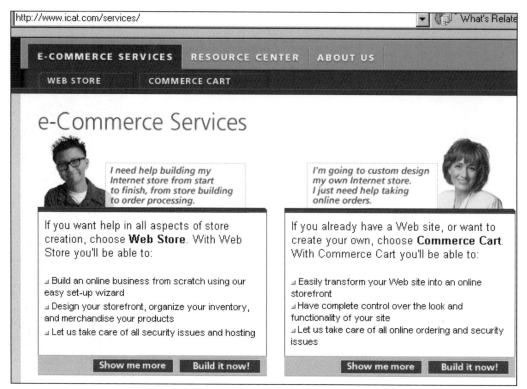

Fig. 45. Icat software offers another solution for people wanting to set up shops online.

It provides merchants the information, technology, and services they need to be successful in ecommerce. The company's award-winning, entry-level ecommerce solution, Commerce Online, is used by thousands of businesses nationwide.

JShop Professional
http://www.jshop.co.uk/pro/
These Manchester-based people are developers of a Javascript shopping basket system for webmasters wanting to incorporate secure online shopping on their sites. The site gives a clear explanation of how it all works, together with ordering information. You can download a 30-day fully-functioning trial of JShop Professional.

Netmedia
http://www.netmedia-uk.com
The UK multimedia company says it was born at the 'start of the internet revolution'. It has since developed a broad range of internet, intranet and web design services for business and education.

Online Design Studios
http://www.online-design-studio.co.uk
This web site creator focuses on meeting the needs of small business wanting a presence on the net. You can explore sample prices, layouts and design styles. They say that clients can decide on the kind of site they want and pay a much lower price without hi tech gobbledygook.

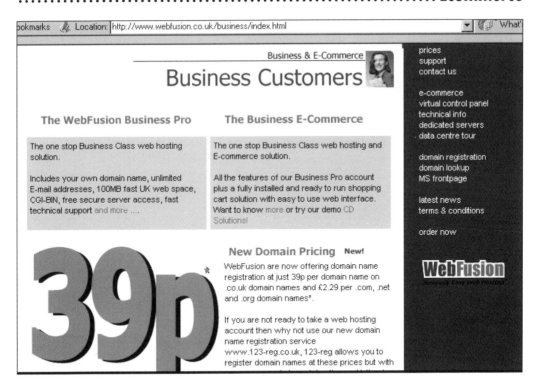

More Internet Handbooks to help you

Building a Web Site on the Internet, Brendan Murphy (2nd edition).
Managing the Internet in Your Organisation, Ian Hosker.
Running a Shop on the Internet, Graham Jones.

9 Using the internet

In this chapter we will explore:

▶ *affiliate and associate opportunities*
▶ *computer manufacturers*
▶ *disability and the internet*
▶ *domain names*
▶ *internet campaigns*
▶ *internet reference*
▶ *internet service providers*
▶ *updating your browser*
▶ *viruses and scams*
▶ *web authoring*
▶ *web development services*

How this chapter can help you

This chapter describes websites which can help you:

1. Explore numerous ways that you can earn money from your web site.

2. Make your site accessible for disabled users.

3. Check out current reviews of affiliate and associate programs.

4. Explore some online computer suppliers.

5. Find registered internet domain names for sale or lease.

6. Get free internet access.

7. Get free monthly updates on scams.

8. Get some computer training, either free or at low cost.

9. Source web site features such as graphics, video, sound, and chat rooms.

10. Access HTML editors, tutorials, banners, guestbooks, clipart and other resources

11. Access an 18,000-page help file about the internet.

12. Obtain free monitoring of search engine results and web log ana-lysis tools.

Affiliate and associate opportunities

Amazon
http://www.amazon.com
Here you can find the leading exponent of the affiliate program, Amazon, the pioneering online bookseller.

Associate Programs UK
http://www.associateprograms.co.uk/
Access a directory of ways webmasters can earn money with their sites. There are hundreds of affiliate links to explore, arranged by subject area. In return for marketing their goods using text and image links, you receive a commission on transactions. The amount you receive varies with each merchant.

ClickQuick
http://www.clickquick.com/
The site contains some useful reviews of various affiliate and associate programs including pay-per-click. There is a clickable list of the ten most popular. They say: 'We like to think of ourselves as the Consumer Reports of affiliate programs, helping webmasters like you find out which programs really work, and which should be avoided.' Each review and rating is based on the overall design of the program, the popularity of the product or service, and feedback from ClickQuick.com visitors.

Fig. 46. Quick Click offers a critical guide to a number of affiliate, pay-per-click, and other potentially revenue-producing programs.

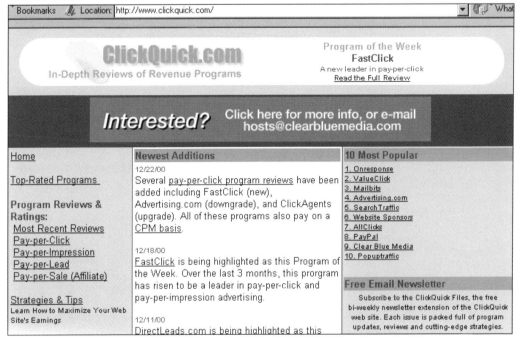

The Affiliate Program
http://theaffiliateprogram.com/
The Affiliate Program Software is an affiliate tracking and management software suite. It includes user-friendly features that could enable you to run your own revenue-sharing affiliate program.

Computer manufacturers

BuyIT Guide
http://www.itworld.co./uk/buyit/index.html
This site is intended for small firms and developed by ITWorld for the DTI's BuyIT best practice group. You can also find some best practice guidelines on electronic commerce and knowledge management.

Compaq Small Business
http://www.compaq.co.uk/prosignia/
Compaq remains one of the most popular personal computers on the market.

Dell Small Business
http://www.euro.dell.com/countries/uk/enu/bsd/default.htm
Dell is the computer system of choice for many business users. The company sells direct.

Gateway
http://www.gateway2000.co.uk/business/businesssplash.htm

IBM Business Computing
http://32.97.242.18/businesscentre/uk/sb3ukpub.nsf/detailcontacts/Home7C72?OpenDocument

Microsoft Small Business
http://www.microsoft.com/uk/business

Fig. 47. The Microsoft UK portal for business customers. It provides access to lots of resources to help you discover how new technology can benefit your business.

Disability and the internet

Bobby
http://www.cast.org/bobby/
Is your site accessible for disabled users? This engine will help you make sure it is.

Computability Centre
http://www.abilitynet.co.uk
On these pages, you'll find a registered charity offering advice and information about computers for disabled people.

Domain names

A-Z Domains
http://www.domaina-z.com/
Registered internet domain names are available here for sale or lease.

Domain Name Analyser
http://freesoftwaretools.com/software.shtm
This program helps you choose a suitable name based on key words that you type in. It will also check WHOIS databases to see if the suggested names are actually available.

Fig. 48. Net Names is one of several sites that enable you to search the availability of domain names worldwide, and then to register your chosen domain names anywhere in the world.

Domain Name Registration
http://www.nic.uk

Domain Names
http://www.netnames.co.uk

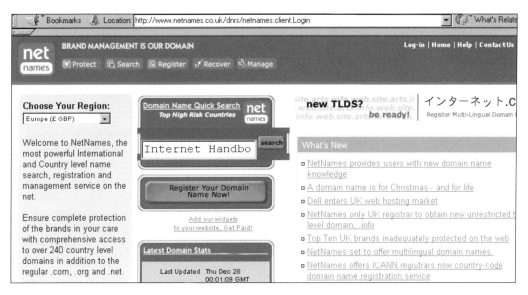

Freenetname ITG
http://www.freenetname.co.uk

InterNames UK
http://www.internames.uk.com/flashframe.htm
This site specialises in the sale of distinctive uk.com domain names that add marketable value to business web sites.

Network Solutions
http://www.networksolutions.com/
This organisation is the prime domain names registration company in the United States. It has registered more than 10 million different web site names. However, all sites in the USA have to be collated by Internic, an official body that ensures that the domain names match the internet protocol numbers.

Nominet
http://www.nominet.org.uk
In the UK, there is only one domain names registrar, Nominet. You can find out more about the procedure here. Like other registrars, Nominet has the authority to accept or reject domain name applications. There is lots of small print associated with domain name applications and you need to be aware of some of these considerations when making your choice.

Internet campaigns

Electronic Frontier Foundation
http://www.eff.org
This respected body campaigns for free speech on the internet (the Blue Ribbon Campaign). It opposes moves by national governments almost everywhere towards increased internet censorship and surveillance. It maintains a large international news archive, including one covering news, events and legislation in the UK.

IT for All
http://www.itforall.org.uk
IT for All is a national campaign that aims to break down the barriers to computer literacy. It seeks to give people of all ages and in all walks of life the confidence and skills to use computers and the internet. IT for All operates through a network of more than 3,000 local centres, most of them based in libraries, schools and colleges, training centres and community groups. All of these centres offer members of the public the opportunity to try out new technology in a friendly environment, either free or at low cost.

Internet reference

Desktop Internet Reference
http://www.vonl.com/vtab24/deskref.htm
This is an enormous 18,000 page Windows help file, covering what
the internet is, what resources are available, how to get them, and
where to find out more.

Kleper Report – Digital Publishing
http://www.printerport.com/kdp/
You can subscribe to a free monthly email newsletter covering DTP
and the internet through this home page.

Internet service providers

America Online
http://www.aol.co.uk
AOL is somewhat different from other ISPs, in that it makes a great
feature of its own online services, and comes with its own proprietary
browser rather than Internet Explorer or Netscape (which it now
owns).

BT Internet
http://www.btclick.com

CompuServe
http://www.compuserve.co.uk

Clara Net
http://www.clara.net

Demon
http://www.demon.net

Freeserve
http://www.freeserve.net
The UK's largest service provider in terms of subscriber numbers,
originally set up by the Dixons/PC World retail chain.

MSN FreeWeb
http://www.msnfreeweb.co.uk
The internet service run by Microsoft Network.

Net4Nowt
http://www.net4nowt.com/
The site contains an excellent guide and links to a large number of
local internet service providers – well worth a look.

Using the internet ....

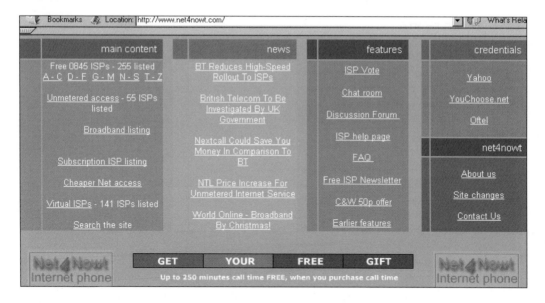

Bookmarks	Location: http://www.net4nowt.com/		What's Rela

main content	news	features	credentials
Free 0845 ISPs - 255 listed A - C D - F G - M N - S T - Z	BT Reduces High-Speed Rollout To ISPs	ISP Vote	Yahoo
Unmetered access - 55 ISPs listed	British Telecom To Be Investigated By UK Government	Chat room	YouChoose.net
Broadband listing	Nextcall Could Save You Money In Comparison To BT	Discussion Forum ISP help page	Oftel
Subscription ISP listing		FAQ	net4nowt
Cheaper Net access	NTL Price Increase For Unmetered Internet Service	Free ISP Newsletter	About us Site changes
Virtual ISPs - 141 ISPs listed	World Online - Broadband By Christmas!	C&W 50p offer	Contact Us
Search the site		Earlier features	

Net4Nowt Internet phone	GET	YOUR	FREE	GIFT	Net4Nowt Internet phone
	Up to 250 minutes call time FREE, when you purchase call time				

Fig. 49. Net4Nowt is an excellent site to explore if you are thinking of choosing or changing an internet service provider.

UK Service Providers
http://www.limitless.co.uk/inetuk/table-provider.html
This is a useful point of reference for British internet service providers.

Virgin Net
http://www.virgin.net
Part of the Richard Branson group of companies.

Which? Online
http://www.which.net

Updating your browser

Microsoft Internet Explorer
http://www.microsoft.com/windows/ie/default.htm
You can download the latest version of the Internet Explorer browser from Microsoft with an idiot-proof guide on how to do it from this site. Be warned: this is a big piece of software and it could take you an hour or more to download it assuming all goes well. There is also news of other technical developments at Microsoft.

Netscape Navigator
http://live.netscape.com/comprod/mirror/clientdownload.html
If you prefer to browse the internet using Netscape Navigator rather than Internet Explorer, you can download the software from here. If you are planning to have your own web site, it is a good idea to check how the site appears when viewed in both Internet Explorer and Netscape, to keep all your clients happy. Between them these two products account for around 90 per cent of the popular browser market.

Viruses and scams

IBM's Antivirus Online
http://www.ibm.com/research/antivirus
The site contains information about IBM anti-virus research activities
and scientific papers.

McAfee
http://www.mcafee.com
McAfee is another well-established supplier of anti-virus software. A
number of other popular computer security products area available
from its online store, including Dr Solomon's Anti-Virus Toolkit and
PGP encryption software.

Norton Antivirus
http://www.symantec.com/nav/
Norton Antivirus is one of the most used and thorough scanning tools
available, produced by Symantec. You can use the web site to obtain
technical support, disk and manual replacements and more. The product is available for both PC and Mac users.

Fig. 50. Norton anti-
virus software. This page
will give you access to
the type of software
protection that no
computer user today can
afford to be without.
Check out the Enterprise
Security Resource
Centre, too.

ScamBusters
http://www.scambusters.org
Free monthly updates on scams and urban legends are available
through this popular site. It has been run as a public service for more
than five years.

Web authoring

Adobe Pagemill
http://www.adobe.com
Adobe Pagemill is a popular WYSIWYG HTML web editor. You can
easily switch design between WYSIWYG and raw HTML, to choose
the design mode that suits you best. You will only need to know a little
HTML to use Adobe Pagemill. It comes with lots of images, sounds
and animated images that you can incorporate into your web pages.

AOLPress
http://www.aolpress.com
AOLPress comes from the giant online service provider America
Online. Pages created using AOLPress will work in any browser and
through any internet service provider. AOLPress suits all levels of
expertise from beginner to web design expert. As well as a web
design package it is a browser, enabling you to view web pages
before you upload them.

Arachnophobia
http://www.arachnoid.com
Available free, Arachnophobia offers lots of functionality and flexibility. You can preview changes as you go along. You can also toggle
between six other browsers, to make sure that your web pages will
work with each of them. Arachnophobia also conveniently lets you
insert pre-formatted text and tables from most Windows-type applications. The package includes some built in FTP software for
uploading your finished pages to the web.

Guestbook
http://www.thefreesite.com/guestresource.htm
Find out how to give your site a guestbook using this site.

Gumball Tracker
http://www.gumball-tracker.com
Gumball is an invisible web site tracker that allows webmasters to
create unique web site traffic reports based on their own specifica-
tions.

HomeSite
http://www.allaire.com/products/homesite/
Produced by Allaire, HomeSite is a well-regarded web authoring
package, used by many professional web developers as well as by
enthusiasts and non-professionals. It offers a WYSIWYG approach to
web design – what you see is what you get. You can fairly easily
develop sites using HTML, DHTML, SMIL, and JavaScript views
before switching to the visual design mode for further tweaking of
your handiwork. It includes some useful wizards – a table and frames

wizard, and a link-verification wizard. It also checks your hyperlinks and HTML code. The package also has a function called Site View, which offers a handy overview of all the files that your web site consists of.

HotDog
http://www.sausage.com
Sausage Software's comprehensive HTML editor includes such features as automatic tag completion, tag error highlighting, and wizards for some of the more involved aspects of coding HTML effectively.

Hyperbanner's QuickBanner Banner Creation Tool
http://www.quickbanner.com
If you want to design a banner for your web site without purchasing software, you can do it online here.

Ipswitch
http://www.ipswitch.com
From here you can download the popular software package WS_FTP which you can use to quickly upload your new web pages to your web host. The acronym stands for 'Windows file transfer protocol'.

Kemosabe's Font Source
http://www.fontaddict.com/home.html
You can access some interesting typefaces through this site.

Macromedia Dreamweaver
http://www.macromedia.com
At under £200, Dreamweaver is used by many professional web

Fig. 51. Macromedia produces an excellent web-authoring package called Dreamweaver. It is now available in version 4.

designers. It comes with templates designed for the small business as well as personal users. It allows the creation of HTML either in WYSIWYG mode or in raw HTML. You can watch the software actually creating the HTML while you type in WYSIWYG mode. Dreamweaver integrates with the excellent Fireworks Studio for creating web images.

Mailloop
http://www.mailloop.com
Through this site, you can access software designed to deliver bulk email. There is a demo version for free download.

MediaBuilder Animated Banner Maker
http://www.mediabuilder.com/abm.html
If you want to design a banner without buying any software, you can do it online here.

Microsoft FrontPage
http://www.microsoft.com/frontpage/
Microsoft FrontPage is probably the world's most popular web authoring package. It enables you to work with frames and to incorporate a range of readymade interactive features. Your internet service provider or web host will need to be able to handle Microsoft Front-Page extensions – not all do, so check first.

NewApps Graphics & Multimedia
http://www.newapps.com/categories.html#category4
There's an up-to-date list of new tools for video, sound, and graphics available on this site.

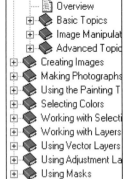

Paint Shop Pro
http://www.jasc.com
Paint Shop Pro enables you to handle the graphic elements of your web site such as GIFs and JPEGs. The current version costs around £70. You can retouch, repair, and edit photos, create your own web graphics and animations using built-in drawing and text tools, add custom images to your home and business graphics, expand your creativity with over 75 special effects, and share photos electronically with friends and family by email and web sites.

ProTrack
http://www.affiliatesoftware.net
This site offers affiliate sales-tracking software. They say their product can increase your internet sales, attract more traffic to your web site, improve your search engine rankings, and automate the tracking and payment of your affiliates.

QuickChat
http://www.quickchat.org
Find out how to add a chat room to your site via this web site. They say: 'Using our advanced QuickChat Code Generator, you can add a java chat applet on your page with minimal work. Just copy and paste the code on your page, and your chat is all set up.'

Really Big
http://reallybig.com/default.shtml
Through these pages you can access various HTML editors, tutorials and other resources plus 3,000 images including free clip art, backgrounds, icons and buttons.

HotMetal Pro
http://www.sq.com
Produced by SoftQuad, HotMetal Pro is another popular web authoring package that solidly occupies the middle ground with good WYSIWYG (what you see is what you get) and HTML features. It is well suited for any small to medium size web project.

Streaming Media World
http://www.streamingmediaworld.com
Just about everything you need to help you put audio and video on your homepage can be found here including tutorials, shareware and commercial tools.

Fig. 52. Submit-It offers a commercial service for everyone wanting to register their domain names with hundreds of top search engines.

Submit it!
http://www.submit-it.com
When your site is ready, you will want to submit its address and other

details to internet search engines. Submit It should be able do this job for you quickly, efficiently and economically. They say: 'In just three short steps you can get submitted to your choice of up to 400 search engines and directories, all for only $59 per year.' The site is maintained by bCentral, a division of Microsoft.

SuperScripts
http://www.superscripts.com
If you are ambitious to make your site more interactive, you can access a variety of practical scripts at this site. It offers ecommerce CGI scripts, dating software, password software, security tools, promotional tools and affiliate software with nearly 60 scripts available online.

UltraEdit-32
http://www.idmcomp.com/products/index.html
This is an ASCII based word processing program offering features for those publishing email newsletters or discussion groups.

Wav Central
http://www.wavcentral.com/index.html
Do you want to add audio files to add to your web site? Wav is the filename extension for a type of sound file. You will find Wav Central a useful source of downloadable audio files including a whole range of special effects from recorded voice messages to pistol shots.

Web Builder
http://www.netmag.co.uk/webbuilder/default.asp
This UK magazine's site deals with every possible aspect of putting together a site, from the tools you need and HTML to Java Script and graphics. Suitable for the beginner and intermediate user.

The How-to Library:

📁 Authoring
📁 Design
📁 Multimedia
📁 E-Business

Webmonkey
http://www.webmonkey.com
This is one of the best-known sites for web developers. It is packed with advice and step-by-step tutorials on how to create a web site using HTML, tables, frames, browsers, style sheets, JavaScript, web authoring software packages and lmore.

WinZip
http://www.winzip.com
WinZip is easy-to-use software for handling compressed files. You can download the software from here in a few minutes. The WinZip Wizard is ideal for the rapidly growing number of PC users getting started with zip files. When these users gain confidence, or want to use more advanced zipping features, the full WinZip Classic interface is just a click away.

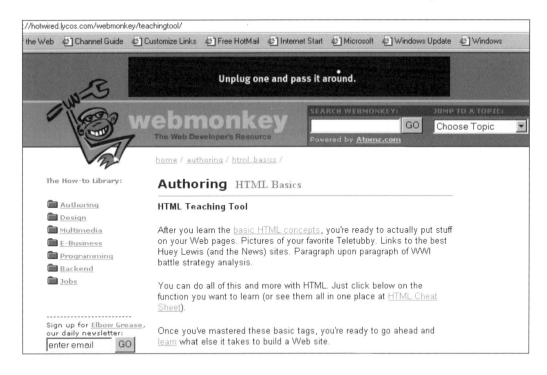

Web development services

Websites Build Business
http://www.websitesbuildbusiness.co.uk/small-biz/web-guide.htm
This is a web guide for UK small businesses, the self-employed and home-workers. They say: 'We hope to include all those topics that could help you to make best use of the net as a small business or self-employed person, particularly those working from home.'

Web Trends
http://www.webtrends.com
Web Trends is one of the better-known commercial services you can use for monitoring and analysing the traffic on your web site.

Web Wise
http://www.bbc.co.uk/webwise/
This is a beginners' guide to the web produced by the BBC Education Unit – 'everything you need to know to make the most of the internet'.

More Internet Handbooks to help you

Building a Web Site on the Internet, Brendan Murphy
Creating a Home Page on the Internet, Richard Cochrane
Free Stuff on the Internet, Kye Valongo
Getting Connected to the Internet, Ian Hosker

Fig. 53. Web Monkey is an established and well-regarded source of tutorials and support, suitable for all levels of web page authoring.

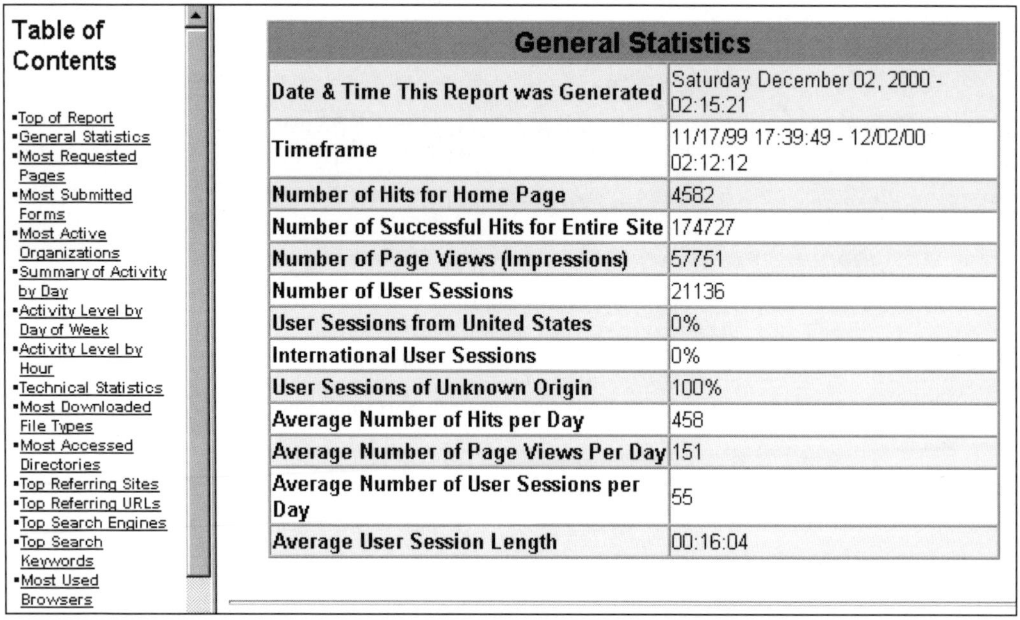

Using the internet ....

**Table of
Contents**

- Top of Report
- General Statistics
- Most Requested Pages
- Most Submitted Forms
- Most Active Organizations
- Summary of Activity by Day
- Activity Level by Day of Week
- Activity Level by Hour
- Technical Statistics
- Most Downloaded File Types
- Most Accessed Directories
- Top Referring Sites
- Top Referring URLs
- Top Search Engines
- Top Search Keywords
- Most Used Browsers

General Statistics

Date & Time This Report was Generated	Saturday December 02, 2000 - 02:15:21
Timeframe	11/17/99 17:39:49 - 12/02/00 02:12:12
Number of Hits for Home Page	4582
Number of Successful Hits for Entire Site	174727
Number of Page Views (Impressions)	57751
Number of User Sessions	21136
User Sessions from United States	0%
International User Sessions	0%
User Sessions of Unknown Origin	100%
Average Number of Hits per Day	458
Average Number of Page Views Per Day	151
Average Number of User Sessions per Day	55
Average User Session Length	00:16:04

Fig. 54. WebTrends is one of the best-known providers of web traffic analysis software.

More Internet Handbooks to help you (continued)

Getting Started on the Internet, Kye Valongo
Internet Explorer on the Internet, Kye Valongo
Naming a Web Site on the Internet, Graham Jones
Using Email on the Internet, Kye Valongo
Where to Find it on the Internet, Kye Valongo (2nd edition).
Your Privacy on the Internet, Kye Valongo

124

10 Telecommuting and homeworking

In this chapter we will explore:

▶ *telecommuting*
▶ *homeworking*

. . . .

How this chapter can help you

The web sites reviewed in this section can help you:

1. Find guidance and advice for setting up your home office.

2. Explore various global internet portals for telework and telecommuting.

3. Get advice on how to approach teleworking technology and opportunities.

4. Explore telecommuting with employers anywhere in the world.

5. Find out about vocational qualifications and training for telework skills.

6. Announce your services and skills to prospective clients or employers.

Telecommuting

BT Working from Home
http://www.wfh.co.uk
Whether you are already working from home, or just thinking about it, this site will help you make the most of the liberating possibilities of telework. It offers guidance and advice for setting up your home office, as well as resources that can help you from day to day. Basic ideas for setting up the technology in your home office are covered in the Home Life section Technology Considerations. The site also discusses some more advanced options that could make your day-to-day work easier.

European Telework Online
http://www.eto.org.uk
This is a useful internet portal for teleworking, telecommuting, and related topics. It contains links to more than 2,500 places across the internet world wide. It publishes the *European IT Observatory* (EITO), an annual reference to European and world use of information and communications technologies.

Flexibility
http://www.flexibility.co.uk
Lots of telecommuting links are available here. Through this site you

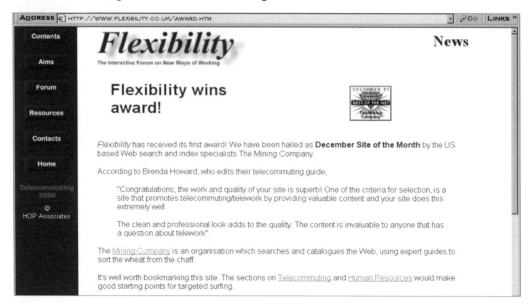

Fig. 55. Flexibility. Visit the section on telecommuting for an insight into new ways of working.

can gain access to consultants who specialise in all aspects of new ways of working. The partnership offers some innovative information technology and telecoms solutions and human resources strategies. It also publishes a newsletter called *Flexibility Online*. The site is run by HOP Associates of Cambridge, and includes some interesting case studies about flexible working practices.

TCA

http://www.tca.org.uk

The TCA claims to be Europe's largest organisation dedicated to the promotion of teleworking. The acronym derives from Telework, Tele-

Fig. 56. The TCA, an organisation for teleworkers.

centre and Telecottage Association. Over 2,000 people and organisations have joined this not-for-profit organisation since it began life in 1993. The TCA provides advice on how to approach teleworking, information about technology, examples of how other people progress, and information about work opportunities. In its bi-monthly magazine *Teleworker*, and in a weekly electronic bulletin, the TCA sends out updates and information about full-time and temporary telework opportunities. It also publishes *The Teleworking Handbook*, a 352-page resource developed with assistance from Lloyds Bank, BT, Hewlett-Packard and other sponsors.

Telecommuting Jobs
http://tjobs.com
From the home page of this site, you can explore telecommuting with employers just about anywhere in the world. There are opportunities for example for artists, writers, web designers, data entry staff, desktop publishers, engineers, programmers, sales people and photographers. You will also find links to an online newsletter and various other useful resources. You can view 60,000 telecommuting work-from-home opportunities, and enter your CV details.

Fig. 57. Telecommuting Jobs. You can explore current telecommuting opportunities, post your CV, and pick up some work tips.

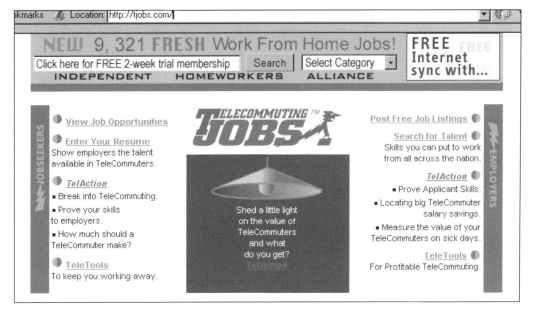

Telelink Training for Europe
http://www.marble.ac.uk/telep/telework/tlpfolder/tlp.html
The TTE project is a European Community (Euroform) funded project which seeks to develop training opportunities in the field of teleworking. The Telework for Europe project aims to establish transnational, vocational qualifications and training for telework skills. This project has already defined a level II Restricted Vocational Qualification

Telecommuting and homeworking.......................................

(RVQ) for teleworkers. The TTE project has set up a network of tele-cottages and training centres around Europe designed to provide training support and service points for telework skills. It has also developed a level III National Vocational Qualification (NVQ) for tele-worker supervisors, and is currently defining a level IV Vocational Qualification for telecottage managers.

Teleweb
http://toucan-europe.co.uk/projects/teleweb/index.html
Teleweb aims to provide support on the web in a manner that is easy to understand and access. Although there is a fair amount of informa-tion available about teleworking, there is a concern that teleworkers may not be able to obtain the support they require. Teleweb aims to tackle this by providing a one-stop location for this support.

Telmet
http://www.telmet.org/
The Telmet project, part-funded by the European Commission, aims to build an open and flexible training methodology in the field of teleworking, designed to suit the needs of training organisations and persons in a variety of occupations wanting access to this new method of working. There are links to training initiatives and other resources. The project is based in Madrid.

Telework Training Resources
http://www.icbl.hw.ac.uk/telep/telework/ttrfolder/typfolder/
typ.html
The directory section is designed to provide teleworkers with a direc-tory for information on various telework organisations, associations, projects and services. It covers the UK and Europe.

Teleworkers at AOL
http://members.aol.com/telework/
Run by the online service provider America Online, this is a commu-nity set up for people who work from home, people who are self employed, and people involved in running small businesses. The Forum is open to all AOL subscribers but only those who have an AOL account can gain access to the benefits provided for its telework community. If you want to find out more about teleworking, working for yourself, working in a small business, you can follow the link from here to a web site called The World of Work:

http://www.telework.org.uk.

Teleworkers Website
http://members.aol.com/telwebsite/index.htm
TWS provides a central location for UK teleworkers to announce their services and skills to prospective employers or clients for free. Any

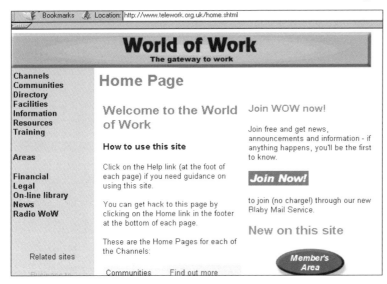

Fig. 58. The Telework web site.

teleworker based in the UK can ask for their details be placed on this site free of charge. You will be placed in an appropriate category decided by the services you offer free of charge. You may make a small voluntary donation (no more than £5) to cover the costs of editing, uploading and maintaining the site if you wish. There are no commissions or other charges payable by you or any employer if any work or contracts are obtained through the site.

Teleworking

http://www.netway.co.uk/users/teleworking.services/
This site provides information and services on teleworking, remote working, finding work and working from home.

Fig. 59. Teleworking. From the fingertips of a real-life teleworker, these pages offer some useful pathways into this method of working.

Telecommuting and homeworking.....................................

Teleworking Web Directory
http://www.users.zetnet.co.uk/maac/myron/telework/twwdir.htm
You can find lots of useful teleworking links on this simple home page.

Homeworking

The web sites reviewed in this section can help you:

1. Find, operate, and expand a work at home business or an online home-based career.

2. Avoid homeworking scams.

3. Subscribe to business and social networks for people who work from home.

4. Explore software, books, shareware and other tools for working at home.

Her Home Office
http://www.herhomeoffice.com
Her Home Office is a one-stop resource for finding, running, operating, expanding and starting a work at home business or an online home-based career. It covers how to start and operate your own home-based business, a basic business model, designing your own web site, starting a consulting business, home-based business ideas for women, making money from online auctions, low-cost home based business opportunities, service businesses you could start, multi-level marketing enterprises, understanding costs and pricing, writing for money, mystery shopping, and assembling products at home.

Home Business Alliance
http://www.homebusiness.org.uk
The HBA works for thousands of people with home-based enterprises. It can offer you a constant supply of valuable, time-saving and quality information to help you achieve your business aims. You will be plugged into a network of experienced advisors including accountants, marketing and business consultants, financial advisors, ex-bank managers, educationalists, publishers, authors, tradespeople and craft workers. What's more, the HBA will be working hard to bring your skills to the attention of businesses that are on the lookout for talented people working on their own. The monthly magazine is full of news and information.

Homeworking
http://www.homeworking.com
This UK oriented site is intended for anyone wanting to work at home or already working at home. You will find lots here to get you started,

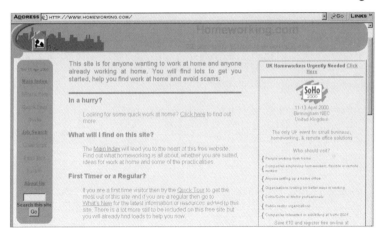

Fig. 60.
Homeworking.com.

to help you find work at home and avoid online pitfalls and scams. Homeworking is a project of Knowledge Computing based in Borehamwood, Hertfordshire.

Homeworking Mom
http://www.homeworkingmom.com
The Mothers' Home Business Network is an organisation which provides ideas, inspiration and support for mothers who choose to work at home. They say: 'You will find lots to get you started, help you find work at home and avoid scams.' Based in the US, and originally founded in 1984, the organisation has around 40,000 users.

Internet Homeworking Directory
http://members.tripod.co.uk/homeworking/
This site deals specifically with UK-based opportunities. These include computing, proofreading, writing, translation, secretarial services, mystery shopping and research, television and film contacts and courses.

Ownbase
http://www.ownbase.org.uk/ownbase.html
OwnBase is an established business and social network. It has been providing a national business and social network since 1986. Membership is open to anyone who works from home (whether employed by an organisation or self-employed), as well as anyone interested in home working or the home-based economy. It publishes six newsletters a year, giving advice and information on business matters, advertising members' services, putting members in touch with each other and organising seminars on homeworking. OwnBase is a voluntary organisation, run by its members, for its members. They say: 'Getting actively involved means you'll get to know like-minded people who could become your clients or suppliers as well as your friends.'

Telecommuting and homeworking.....................................

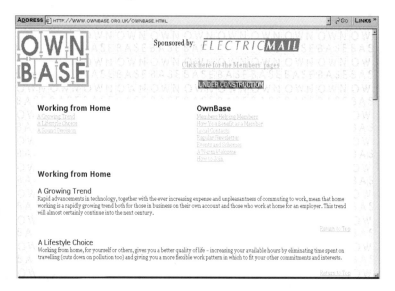

Fig. 61. Ownbase has established itself as one of the best-known UK organisations for homeworkers. When you visit its site you might decide to join up to the growing trend of working from home.

Work at Home
http://www.visitorinfo.com/Work-At-Home/WorkAt-Home-Center.htm
The Work At Home Self-Employment Centre presents information on software, books, shareware and other needed work at home self-employment needs. It offers videos, mailing lists and business opportunities of various kinds.

Working From Home
http://www.home-workers.com/
This is an electronic edition of *All About Working From Home* magazine. It offers a menu of news, features and advice for those who have swapped the rat race for the comfort of the home office.

Fig. 62. The Home-Workers.com

More Internet Handbooks to help you

Finding a Job on the Internet, Brendan Murphy (2nd edition).
Getting Connected to the Internet, Ian Hosker.
Getting Started on the Internet, Kye Valongo.
Internet Skills for the Workplace, Ian Hosker.
Where to Find It on the Internet, Kye Valongo (2nd edition).

11 Education and training online

In this chapter we will explore:

▶ the BBC's record-and-play service for students
▶ cyber-coaching
▶ online distance and open education and training options
▶ free advice on effective learning and career development
▶ the University for Industry (UFI) project

BBC Learning Zone
http://www.bbc.co.uk/education/lzone/
This site supports BBC 2's overnight record-and-play service for online learners. There is a great variety of student subjects on offer every night, from languages to technology, computing to the environment and links for all ages and interests. A BBC Learning Zone Programme Guide is available from here.

BUBL Links
http://www.bubl.ac.uk/link

Fig. 63. Run by qualified librarians, BUBL Link offers a quick means of exploring academic courses in higher education in the UK.

BUBL is the name of a substantial UK library-based catalogue of selected internet resources covering all academic subject areas. All items are evaluated, catalogued and described. Links are checked and fixed each month. BUBL LINK is the name of a catalogue of selected internet resources covering all academic subject areas and catalogued according to DDC (Dewey Decimal Classification). LINK stands for Libraries of Networked Knowledge. See under Social

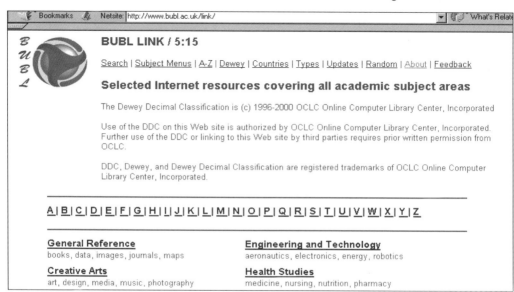

Bookmarks   Netsite: http://www.bubl.ac.uk/link/   What's Relate

BUBL LINK / 5:15

Search | Subject Menus | A-Z | Dewey | Countries | Types | Updates | Random | About | Feedback

Selected Internet resources covering all academic subject areas

The Dewey Decimal Classification is (c) 1996-2000 OCLC Online Computer Library Center, Incorporated

Use of the DDC on this Web site is authorized by OCLC Online Computer Library Center, Incorporated. Further use of the DDC or linking to this Web site by third parties requires prior written permission from OCLC.

DDC, Dewey, and Dewey Decimal Classification are registered trademarks of OCLC Online Computer Library Center, Incorporated.

A | B | C | D | E | F | G | H | I | J | K | L | M | N | O | P | Q | R | S | T | U | V | W | X | Y | Z

General Reference
books, data, images, journals, maps

Creative Arts
art, design, media, music, photography

Engineering and Technology
aeronautics, electronics, energy, robotics

Health Studies
medicine, nursing, nutrition, pharmacy

Sciences for business links. The BUBL LINK catalogue currently holds over 11,000 resources. This is smaller than the databases held by major search engines, but it can often provide a more effective route to information for particular subjects, across all disciplines.

CyberCoach
http://www.cybercoach.org.uk
CyberCoach is a service that works anonymously over the web. You can have access to MBA standard executive coaching at a fraction of the cost of a visiting executive coach. You don't have to reveal your business or yourself if you do not wish to. To discover whether it is going to work for you, you receive your first consultation free.

Distance Learning
http://www.distance-learning.co.uk
This is an online service called Distance Learning in Association with The Open University. It contains details of international distance and open education and training, using a large global database of distance and open learning courses. You can choose details of courses on: accountancy, finance and economics, applied science, arts and humanities building and planning, business and administration, communications, computer science and information technology, education and training, examinations, law, leisure, management, medicine, pure science and maths and social sciences.

Distance Learning on the Net
http://www.hoyle.com/distance.htm
This is a useful page of links for online and distance learning. Included are descriptions of distance education web sites, along with links to lead you to further distance learning and education resources on the net.

HTML Writers Guild
http://www.hwg.org
The site includes online training courses for people wanting learn to write hypertext markup language, or to brush up their skills in this area.

International Centre for Distance Learning
http://www-icdl.open.ac.uk
This is a site originated by the Open University. The ICDL is an international centre for research, teaching, consultancy, information and publishing activities. From its home page you can access databases on literature, institutions and courses. There icons to contact the Open University and the ICDL. You can find out how to get a qualification in Open and Distance Education. One icon on the home page will take you to ICDL services. Another will take you to a bulletin board, while another will take you to collaborative projects.

Education and training online ....

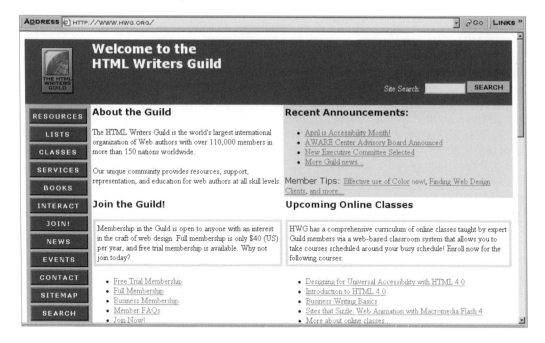

Welcome to the HTML Writers Guild

THE HTML WRITERS GUILD

Site Search: [_____] SEARCH

RESOURCES

LISTS

CLASSES

SERVICES

BOOKS

INTERACT

JOIN!

NEWS

EVENTS

CONTACT

SITEMAP

SEARCH

About the Guild

The HTML Writers Guild is the world's largest international organization of Web authors with over 110,000 members in more than 150 nations worldwide.

Our unique community provides resources, support, representation, and education for web authors at all skill levels.

Join the Guild!

Membership in the Guild is open to anyone with an interest in the craft of web design. Full membership is only $40 (US) per year, and free trial membership is available. Why not join today?

- Free Trial Membership
- Full Membership
- Business Membership
- Member FAQs
- Join Now!

Recent Announcements:

- April is Accessibility Month!
- AWARE Center Advisory Board Announced
- New Executive Committee Selected
- More Guild news...

Member Tips: Effective use of Color new!, Finding Web Design Clients, and more...

Upcoming Online Classes

HWG has a comprehensive curriculum of online classes taught by expert Guild members via a web-based classroom system that allows you to take courses scheduled around your busy schedule! Enroll now for the following courses:

- Designing for Universal Accessibility with HTML 4.0
- Introduction to HTML 4.0
- Business Writing Basics
- Sites that Sizzle: Web Animation with Macromedia Flash 4
- More about online classes...

Fig. 64. The home page of the HTML Writers Guild. Take a look at its resources, classes and events. You can take out a trial membership.

International School of Information Management
http://www.isimu.edu
The ISIM is an accredited provider of distance education and training. It offers graduate degrees in business administration and information management. In addition to graduate degree programs, it offers corporate training programs, and classes for continuing education in a number of career-enhancing courses for the adult professional. You can use this site to learn more about ISIM and apply for admission online.

JER Group
http://www.jergroup.com
This US-based site offers some online courses for the internet learner; small business internet workshops, technical writing, creative writing, digital graphics and more.

Learn@Hand
http://www.stewartpiper.com/Education.html
Learn@Hand offers web-based training in basic business skills, internet, HTML, advanced programming, networking, and a number of others - around 180 interactive courses in all. Topic areas are diverse and range from internet skills to Microsoft Desktop to professional development and a wide selection of technical training topics.

Learn Direct
http://www.learndirect.co.uk
This site gives access to free advice on learning and career matters. They say: 'We've designed flexible learning packages that you can use as and when you want them. Target each business issue in bite-sized modules. Tailor your learning to meet your business need. Browse through our course catalogue. Take a look at our factsheets. Try a taster of a learndirect course.' There is a free telephone helpline as well (0800 100 900).

National Council for Training of Journalists
http://www.itecharlow.co.uk/nctj/
This is site offers advice on careers and training in journalism.

National Extension College
http://www.nec.ac.uk
The NEC specialises in supported home study courses and learning resources for professionals. The home page presents a multitude of icons. The bright green section is split into three: one with several icons related to NEC (e.g. contacts and equal opportunities), the second column has icons related to its learning programme divisions (e.g. courses and student information) and the third column links you into the learning resources division (e.g. tutor/training resources). The sky blue icons down the left side take you into NEC press releases, partnerships and recruitment. Yet another icon takes you to NEC News.

Fig. 65. The National Extension College. From this home page, you can explore leisure and qualification courses of every shape and size.

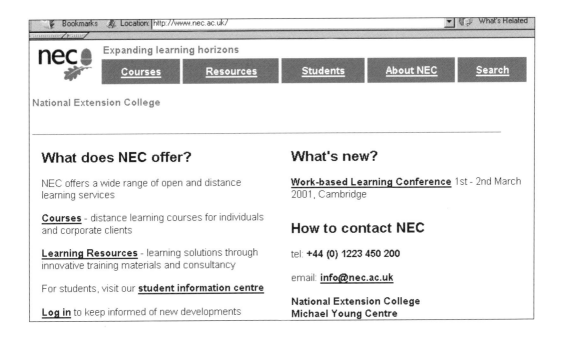

137

Education and training online ....

Online Learning
http://www.onlinelearning.net
Online Learning is a online supplier of continuing higher education, dedicated to providing busy professionals with the tools needed to pursue their lifelong learning objectives. Choose from a wide variety of certificated and sequential online programs and courses designed with your career in mind. Visit the 'available classes' page for more details.

Open University
http://www.open.ac.uk
The OU is Britain's largest and most innovative university. Founded by royal charter in 1969, it has grown rapidly both in student numbers and range of courses. There are professional development programmes in management, education, health and social welfare, manufacturing and computer applications, as well as self-contained study packs.

The Business Information Zone
http://www.thebiz.co.uk
This site is a business directory with access to a virtual training zone which links you to The Virtual Training Calendar (training courses) or The Virtual Training Library (products). There is a search function that takes you into pages of further links related to your chosen area. For each title you will find pricing details, a short description of the product or service and an enquiry form for further information.

Training and Enterprise Councils
http://www.tec.co.uk
This site page provides links to the local TEC headquarters around the country.

University for Industry (Learndirect)
http://www.ufiltd.co.uk
UFI describes itself as a new kind of public-private partnership that aims to boost the competitiveness of business and the employability of individuals. Working with businesses and education and training providers, it plans to use modern technologies to make learning available at a time and place to suit the learner - at home, in the workplace and through a national network of learning centres.

Virtual Business University
http://www.virtualbusinessu.com
VBU is a virtual university dedicated to teaching business owners how to use the internet as a business tool. It makes use of teleclasses: you can dial into a telephone number that connects you to what they call a teleconference bridge. This virtual classroom holds anywhere from 2 to 30 participants from all over the world and is live and interactive.

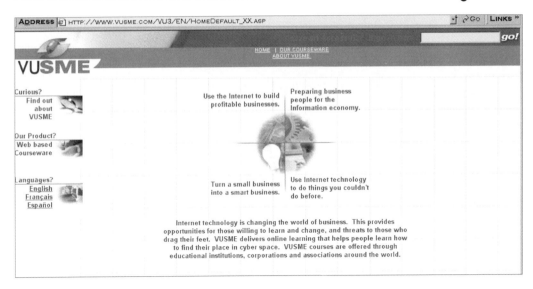

HOME | OUR COURSEWARE
ABOUT VUSME

VUSME

Curious?
Find out
about
VUSME

Our Product?
Web based
Courseware

Languages?
English
Français
Español

Use the Internet to build profitable businesses.

Preparing business people for the Information economy.

Turn a small business into a smart business.

Use Internet technology to do things you couldn't do before.

Internet technology is changing the world of business. This provides opportunities for those willing to learn and change, and threats to those who drag their feet. VUSME delivers online learning that helps people learn how to find their place in cyber space. VUSME courses are offered through educational institutions, corporations and associations around the world.

Virtual University for Small and Medium Sized Enterprises
http://www.vusme.com
The Virtual University for small and medium enterprises uses courses and case studies to help entrepreneurs use the internet to start and grow profitable business.

Writing School
http://www.writingschool.com
This is an online college-level school that specialises in teaching all aspects of writing: fiction, non-fiction, business writing, screenwriting, and academic writing. The instructors are experienced writers and teachers.

More Internet Handbooks to help you

Careers Guidance on the Internet, Laurel Alexander.
Education & Training on the Internet, Laurel Alexander.
Internet For Schools, Barry Thomas & Richard Williams.
Internet For Students, David Holland (reprinted).
Where to Find It on the Internet, Kye Valongo (2nd edition).

Fig. 66. The Virtual University for Small and Medium Sized Enterprises. Have a look at this site's web-based courseware. You can even choose the language to view it in.

12 Finding out more online

In this chapter we will explore

▶ *searching the internet*
▶ *tips for searching*
▶ *bookmarking your favourite web sites*
▶ *search engines and directories*
▶ *search utilities and resources*

Searching the internet

The usual way to look up something on the internet is to go to the web site of a well-known search engine or internet directory. These services are free and open to everyone.

▶ *Search engines* – These are also known as spiders or crawlers. They have highly sophisticated search tools that automatically seek out web sites across the internet. These trawl through and index literally millions of pages of internet content. As a result they often find information that is not listed in traditional directories.

▶ *Internet directories* – These are developed and compiled by people, rather than by computers. Web authors submit their web site details, and these details get listed in the relevant sections of the directory.

The browser that your ISP supplies you with – typically Internet Explorer or Netscape - should include an internet seach facility, ready for you to use, but you are perfectly free to visit any of the search engines listed below, and use them yourself.

Most people refer to directories as search engines and lump the two together. For the purposes of this book, we will refer to them all as search engines. Popular search engines have now become big web sites in their own right, usually combining many useful features. As well as search boxes where you can type key words to summarise what you are looking for, you will usually also find handy directories of information, news, email and many other services. There are hundreds if not thousands of search engines freely available. The biggest and best known are AltaVista, Excite, Google, Infoseek, Lycos and Yahoo! (the most popular of all).

Tips for searching

1. If you want general information, try Yahoo! or AltaVista first. For

specific information, try one or more of the major search engines. After experimenting, many people decide on their own favourite search engine and stick to it most of the time.

2. If you do a search for law careers, the search engine will search for 'law', and search for 'careers' quite separately. This could produce details of engineering careers, for example – not what you want. The way to avoid this is to enclose all your key words inside a pair of quotation marks. If you type in 'law careers' then only web sites with that combination of words should be listed for you.

3. George Boole was a 19th-century English mathematician who worked on logic. He gave his name to Boolean operators - simple words like AND, OR and NOT. If you include these words in your searches, it should narrow down the results, for example: 'marketing AND sales NOT Europe'. However, don't go overboard and restrict the search too much, or you may get few or no results.

4. Try out several different search engines, and see which one you like the best. Or you could obtain the handy little search utility called Web Ferret (see below): if the information is not on one search engine, Web Ferret can usually find it on one or more of the others.

Bookmarking your favourite web sites

Your browser (usually Internet Explorer or Netscape Navigator) enables you to save the addresses of any web sites you specially like, and may want to revisit. These are called Bookmarks in Netscape, or Favorites in Internet Explorer (US spelling). In either case, simply mouse-click on the relevant button on your browser's toolbar – Bookmarks or Favorites as the case may be. This produces a little drop-down menu that you click on to add the site concerned. When you want to revisit that site later, click again on the same button; then click the name of the web site you bookmarked, and within a few seconds it should open for you.

Search engines and directories

AltaVista
http://www.altavista.com
http://www.altavista.co.uk
Alta Vista is one of the most popular search sites among web users world wide. It contains details of millions of web pages on its massive and ever-growing database. You can either follow the trails of links from its home page, or (better) type in your own key words into its search box. You can even search in about 25 different languages.

Finding out more online..

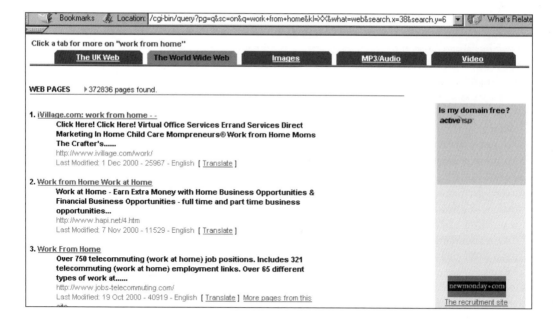

Click a tab for more on "work from home"

| The UK Web | The World Wide Web | Images | MP3/Audio | Video |

WEB PAGES ▶ 372836 pages found.

1. iVillage.com: work from home - -
   Click Here! Click Here! Virtual Office Services Errand Services Direct
   Marketing In Home Child Care Mompreneurs® Work from Home Moms
   The Crafter's......
   http://www.ivillage.com/work/
   Last Modified: 1 Dec 2000 - 25967 - English [Translate]

2. Work from Home Work at Home
   Work at Home - Earn Extra Money with Home Business Opportunities &
   Financial Business Opportunities - full time and part time business
   opportunities...
   http://www.hapi.net/4.htm
   Last Modified: 7 Nov 2000 - 11529 - English [Translate]

3. Work From Home
   Over 750 telecommuting (work at home) job positions. Includes 321
   telecommuting (work at home) employment links. Over 65 different
   types of work at......
   http://www.jobs-telecommuting.com/
   Last Modified: 19 Oct 2000 - 40919 - English [Translate] More pages from this

Is my domain free?
active'rsp'

newmonday•com
The recruitment site

Fig. 67. The very popular search engine AltaVista. Here, the user is carrying out a search for web sites relating to working from home.

Ask Jeeves

http://www.askjeeves.com/

Ask Jeeves offers a slightly different approach to searches. It invites you to ask questions on the internet just as you would of a friend or colleague. For example you could type in something like: 'Where can I find out about marketing?' Jeeves retrieves the information, drawing from a knowledge base of millions of standard answers.

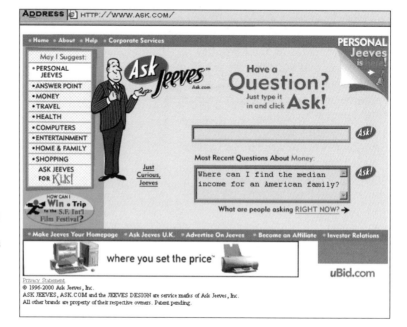

Fig. 68. The Ask search engine features the unflappable manservant from the novels of PG Wodehouse. Ask Jeeves any question, and (in theory) he'll come up with a helpful answer in terms of relevant web site links.

Electronic Yellow Pages
http://www.eyp.co.uk
These electronic yellow pages are organised on the same lines as the paper edition. Just type in the details of the information you need - anything from solicitors to courts - and it quickly searches for appropriate services in your local area.

Excite
http://www.excite.com
http://www.excite.co.uk
Excite is another of the top ten search engines and directories on the internet. To refine your search, simply click the check boxes next to the words you want to add and then click the Search Again button. There are separate Excite home pages for several different countries and cultures including Australia, Chinese, France, German, Italy, Japan, Netherlands, Spain, Sweden, and the USA.

Global On-line Directory
http://www.god.co.uk/
Launched in 1996, GOD is fairly unusual among search engines in that it is UK-based, and aims to be a premier European search service. Features of the site include a 'global search' where you can search for web sites by country, state, province, county or even city by city, narrowing down the information for a more focused result. It you have your own web site, you can submit its address here.

Google
http://www.google.com
A new and innovative search site, popular among busy professional internet users, is Google, which has an easy-to-use no-nonsense format. It matches your query to the text in its index, to find relevant pages. For instance, when analysing a page for indexing, it looks at what the pages linking to that page have to say about it, so the rating partly depends on what others say about it. This highly-regarded search facility has indexed well over a billion pages on the world wide web, and is now helping to power Yahoo!

HotBot
http://hotbot.lycos.com/
This is an impressive, very popular, and well-classified search engine and directory, now associated with Lycos (see below).

Infoseek (Go Network)
http://www.infoseek.co.uk
In 1994, the American 'netpreneur' Steve Kirsch founded Infoseek with the mission of helping people unleash the power of the internet. Infoseek pioneered a suite of powerful, high-quality and easy-to-use search tools. Infoseek is one of the leading search engines on the

internet, and is now teamed up with Disney under the Go brand. This is its main UK page.

Internet Address Finder

http://www.iaf.net/

The IAF is used by millions of web users for searching and finding the names, email addresses, and now Intel Internet videophone contacts, of other users world wide. With more than 6 million addresses it is one of the most comprehensive email directories on the internet. By registering, you will also enable others to find you. The Internet Address Finder is produced by DoubleClick, one of the world's best known internet advertising networks.

Internet Public Library

http://www.ipl.org/ref/

Here you can use the 'ask-a-question' service offered by the Internet Public Library. Your question is received at the IPL Reference Centre and the mail is reviewed once a day and questions are forwarded to a place where all the librarians can see them and answer them. Replies are sent as soon as possible, advising whether your question has been accepted or rejected. If it has been accepted, you should receive an answer to in two to seven days. The librarians who work here are mostly volunteers with other full-time librarian jobs. They say: 'Over the last few hundred years, librarians have become skilled at finding the good stuff, organizing it, and making it easier for people to find and useThe Internet Public Library is the first public library of the internet. As librarians, we are committed to providing valuable services to that world.'

Looksmart

http://www.looksmart.com

This is another good directory with a huge number of catalogued sites. You can find it on the Netscape Net Search Page. If your search is not successful, you are redirected to AltaVista.

Lycos

http://www.lycos.com

http://www.lycos.co.uk

Lycos is another of the top ten worldwide web search engines. Lycos is the name for a type of ground spider ('spider' being the term for a type of search engine). It searches document titles, headings, links, and keywords, and returns the first few words of each page it indexes for your search. Founded in 1995, Lycos was one of the earliest search and navigation sites designed to help people find information more easily and quickly on the world wide web. The core technology was developed at Carnegie Mellon University. Since 1997, with the media giant Bertelsmann, it has launched Lycos sites in 11 European countries.

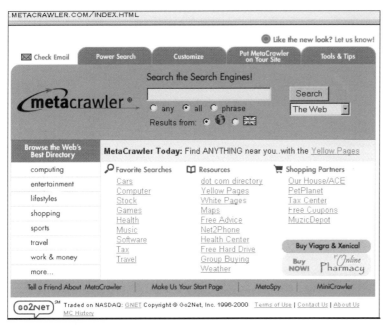

Fig. 69. The Metacrawler search engine. Enter your query, and it will search lots of search engines for you, saving you the bother.

Metacrawler
http://www.metacrawler.com
MetaCrawler was originally developed by Erik Selberg and Oren Et-zioni at the University of Washington, and released to the internet in 1995. In response to each user query, it incorporates results from all the top search engines. It collates results, eliminates duplication, scores the results and provides the user with a list of relevant sites.

SavvySearch
http://www.savvysearch.com
Owned by CNET, SavvySearch is one of the leading providers of metasearch services. Its search engine offers a single point of access to hundreds of different search engines, guides, archives, libraries, and other resources. You type in a keyword query which is then immediately sent out to all appropriate internet search engines. The results are gathered and displayed within a few seconds.

Scoot Yahoo!
http://scoot.yahoo.co.uk
Yahoo! has combined with the British directory Scoot to offer an excellent search facility for those looking for UK-oriented information, businesses and organisations. Once you have found the organisation you are looking for you can click straight into their web site if they have one.

Search.com
http://search.cnet.com/
This service is run by CNET, one of the world's leading new-media

companies. From the home page you can click an A-Z list of options which displays an archive of all its search engines. The list is long, but just about everything you need to master the web is there. You can search yellow pages, phone numbers, email addresses, message boards, software downloads, and easily do all kinds of special searches.

Snap
http://www.snap.com
Snap is run by the media conglomerate NBC and is heavily biased towards the USA. However, it is a quick and easy to use service that is gaining in popularity because it returns search results much faster than much of the competition.

Starting Point MetaSearch
http://www.stpt.com/search.html
This is a powerful metasearcher that puts numerous high-quality, popular, and comprehensive search tools – general and category specific – at your fingertips.

UK Directory
http://www.ukdirectory.co.uk/
This is a useful directory listing to UK-based web sites. You can browse it or search it. It has a well-classified subject listing. UK Directory is simple and intuitive to use. You don't need to know the name of the company, service or person to find the things you are interested in. Just look in the category that best suits your needs. It is as easy to use as a telephone directory.

UK Plus
http://www.ukplus.co.uk/
The parent company of this UK-oriented search engine and database is Daily Mail & General Trust - owners of the *Daily Mail,* the *Mail on Sunday, London Evening Standard* and a number of UK regional newspapers - so it draws on a rich tradition of publishing. It has built up a vast store of web site reviews written by a team of experienced journalists. Although it concentrates on UK web sites, you will also find many from all over the world which are included because it feels they are likely to be of interest to British-based readers.

UK Yellow Web Directory
http://www.yell.co.uk/
This site is operated by the yellow pages division of British Telecom. It is indexed 'by humans' and is searchable. A number of non-UK sites are included in the database. There is also an A to Z company listing, but note that companies whose names begin with 'The' are listed under T. A Business Compass lists 'the best' business internet resources, with links and brief descriptions.

Webcrawler
http://webcrawler.com/
Webcrawler is a fast worker and returns an impressive list of links. It analyses the full text of documents, allowing the searcher to locate key words which may have been buried deep within a document's text. Webcrawler is now part of Excite.

Whois
http://www.whois.net
The site offers a free domain name lookup service, suggest-a-name search, deleted domain search, internet keyword applications, free domain name monitoring, and free trademark search.

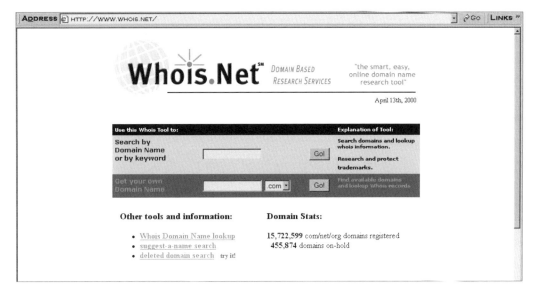

Fig. 70. Whois.Net.

World Email Directory
http://www.worldemail.com/
This site is dedicated to email, email, more email, finding people and locating businesses and organisations. WED has access to an esti-mated 18 million email addresses and more than 140 million business and phone addresses world wide. Here you'll find everything from email software, to email list servers, many world wide email data-bases, business, telephone and fax directories and a powerful email search engine.

Yahoo!
http://www.yahoo.com
http://www.yahoo.co.uk
Yahoo! was the first substantial internet directory, and continues to be one of the best for free general searching. It contains over a billion links categorised by subject. You can 'drill down' through the well-organised categories to find what you want, or you can carry out

Finding out more online..

Web Page Matches   (1 - 20 of about 891000)

- Workplace Substance Abuse
  ... Feedback, About **Working** Partners. Substance Abuse Information Database - SAID. Small Business ... Return to DOL **Home** DOL **Home** Page | Return to Agency **Home** Page OASP ...
  http://www.dol.gov/dol/workingpartners.htm

- BT **Working** From **Home**
  Whether you're already working from home, or just thinking about it, this site will help you make the most of the liberating possibilities of telework. Here ...
  http://www.wfh.co.uk/ [More results from www.wfh.co.uk]

- **Working** Solo **Home** Page
  ... business. And if you're a company that wants to reach the SOHO (small office/**home** office) marketplace, **Working** Solo, Inc., can help you make the connection. ...
  http://www.workingsolo.com/ [More results from www.workingsolo.com]

- TYPIST - MAKE MONEY **WORKING** FROM **HOME**
  [Full List | Reply] TYPIST - MAKE MONEY **WORKING** FROM **HOME** ... Replies from other people:
  Re: TYPIST - MAKE MONEY **WORKING** FROM **HOME** Vikki J. O'Banon - 4/20/100: ...
  http://www.ib3.gmu.edu/bboards/staden/post/30.html [More results from www.ib3.gmu.edu]

- IETF WEBDAV **Working** Group **Home** Page

Fig 71. With well over a billion pages, Yahoo! remains the world's biggest and most consulted internet directory. It has recently joined forces with the well-regarded Google search engine.

your own searches using keywords. The site also offers world news, sport, weather, email, chat, retailing facilities, clubs and many other features. Yahoo! is probably one of the search engines and directories you will use time after time, as do millions of people every day.

Search utilities and resources

Informant
http://informant.dartmouth.edu
The Informant is a free service that will save your favourite search engine queries and web sites, check them periodically, and send you email whenever there are new or updated web pages.

List of Search Engines
http://www.search-engine-index.co.uk
This enterprising British site offers a free list of hundreds of search engines, covering all kinds of different topics. There are software search engines, multiple search engines, email/news search engines, web search engines, commercial search engines, word reference and science search, law search, TV, film and music search, image search, technology manufacturers search, and various localised search engines. Recommended.

Search Engine Colossus
http://www.searchenginecolossus.com
Here you will find one of the biggest collections of links to search engines anywhere in the world. It is organised by country; click on a link to a particular country and your screen will display the top search engines, internet directories and portal sites for that particular country.

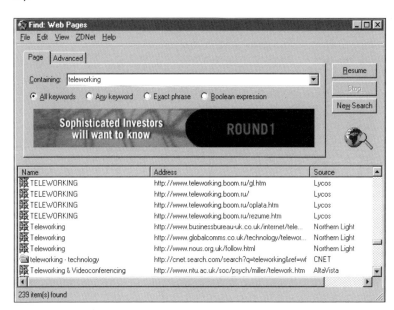

Fig. 72. Web Ferret will speed up and broaden your searches. Here it is being used to search for web sites dealing with teleworking. Once you start using this neat little program, you may wonder how you ever managed without it.

WebFerret
http://www.ferretsoft.com
WebFerret is an excellent functional search utility. You can key in your query offline, and when you connect it searches the web until it has collected all the references you have specified - up to 9,999 if you wish. WebFerret queries ten or more search engines simultaneously and discards any duplicate results. The search engines it queries include AltaVista, Yahoo, Infoseek, Excite, and others. You can immediately visit the web pages it lists for you, even while WebFerret is still running. The trial version of the program is free, and simplicity itself. It only takes a few minutes to download from FerretSoft. Highly recommended.

Other Internet Handbooks to help you

Exploring Yahoo! on the Internet, David Holland.
Finding a Job on the Internet, Brendan Murphy (2nd edition).
Getting Started on the Internet, Kye Valongo.
Internet for Students, David Holland (reprinted).
Where to Find It on the Internet, Kye Valongo (2nd edition).

Further reading

Books

Building a Web Site on the Internet, Brendan Murphy (Internet Handbooks).
Careers Guidance on the Internet, Laurel Alexander (Internet Handbooks).
Creating a Home Page on the Internet, Richard Cochrane (Internet Handbooks).
Finding a Job on the Internet, David Holland (Internet Handbooks).
How To Start A Business from Home, Graham Jones (How To Books).
How To Work From Home, Ian Phillipson (How To Books).
Internet for Writers, Nick Daws (Internet Handbooks).
Making Money from Your Home, Hazel Evans (Piatkus).
Marketing your Business on the Internet, Sara Edlington (Internet Handbooks, 2nd edition).
Small Business Guide to the Internet, Richard G Lewis (Oak Tree Press).
Teleworking Handbook. The new edition of the Handbook is now available as part of membership of the TCA or can be ordered by posting a cheque payable to the Telecottage Association to: Teleworking Handbook, TCA, FREEPOST CV2312, WREN, Kenilworth, Warwickshire, CV8 2RR.
Which? Guide to Earning Money at Home, Lynn Underwood (Which? Publications).

Government publications

The following government publications (both priced and free) are available by mail order from HSE Books, PO Box 1999, Sudbury, Suffolk CO10 6FS. Tel: (0178)7 881165. Fax: (017187) 313995. Priced publications are also available from good bookstores.

Display Screen Equipment Work, Health and Safety Display Screen Equipment Regulations 1992. Guidance on Regulations. ISBN 0 7176 0410.
VDUs: An Easy Guide to the Regulations HS(G)90. ISBN 0 7176 0735 6.
Working with VDUs. IND(G)36L (free).

Monthly magazines

Internet Magazine
http://www.internet-magazine.com

Internet Works
http://www.iwks.com

.Net
http://www.futurenet.com/net/

Glossary of internet terms

access provider – The company that provides you with access to the internet. See also **internet service provider**.

ActiveX – A Microsoft programming language that allows effects such as animations, games and other interactive features to be included a web page.

Adobe Acrobat – A type of software required for reading PDF files ('portable document format').

address book – A directory in a web browser where you can store people's email addresses.

ADSL – Asymmetric Digital Subscriber Line, phone line technology designed to provide a much fast internet connection speed.

AOL – America OnLine, the world's biggest internet service provider, with some 27 million subscribers.

Apple Macintosh – A type of computer that has its own proprietary operating system, as distinct from the MSDOS and Windows operating systems found on PCs (personal computers).

applet – An application programmed in Java that is designed to run only on a web browser.

application – Any program, such as a word processor or spreadsheet program, designed for use on your computer.

ARPANET – Advanced Research Projects Agency Network, an early form of the internet.

ASCII – American Standard Code for Information Interchange. It is a simple text file format that can be accessed by most word processors and text editors.

attachment – A file sent with an email message.

bandwidth – The width of the electronic highway that gives you access to the internet. The higher the bandwidth, the wider this highway, and the faster the traffic can flow.

baud rate – The data transmission speed in a modem, measured in kps (kilobits per second).

BBS – Bulletin board service. A facility to read and to post public messages on a particular web site.

Blue Ribbon Campaign – An internet free speech campaign. See: http://www.eff.org

bookmarks – A file of URLs of your favourite internet sites. In the Internet Explorer browser and AOL they are called Favorites.

boolean search – A search in which you type in words such as AND and OR to refine your search. Such words are called 'Boolean operators'.

bot – Short for robot. It is used to refer to a program that will perform a task on the internet, such as carrying out a search.

browser – Your browser is the program that you use to access the world wide web, and manage your personal communications and privacy when online. By far the two most popular browsers are Netscape Navigator and its dominant rival Microsoft Internet Explorer.

bug – A weakness in a program or a computer system.

bulletin board – A type of computer-based news service that provides an email service and a file archive.

cache – A file storage area on a computer. Your web browser will normally cache (copy to your hard drive) each web page you visit.

certificate – A computer file that securely identifies a person or organisation on the internet.

channel (chat) – Place where you can chat with other internet chatters. The name of a chat channel is prefixed with a hash mark, #.

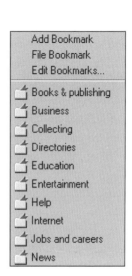

Glossary of internet terms ....

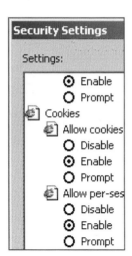

Dial-Up
Networking

client – This is the term given to the program that you use to access the internet. For example your web browser is a web client, and your email program is an email client.

configure – To set up, or adjust the settings, of a computer or software program.

content – The text, articles, images, columns and sales messages of a web site.

cookie – A cookie is a small text code that the server of a web page asks your browser to store on your hard drive. It may be used to store password or registration details, and pass information about your site usage to the web site concerned.

cracker – Someone who breaks into computer systems.

crash – What happens when a computer program malfunctions.

cyberspace – Popular term for the intangible 'place' where you go to surf – the ethereal world of computers and telecommunications on the internet.

data – Information. Data can exist in many forms such as numbers in a spreadsheet, text in a document, or as binary numbers stored in a computer's memory.

database – A store of information in digital form. Many web sites make use of substantial databases to deliver maximum content at high speed to the web user.

dial up account – This allows you to connect your computer to your internet provider's computer remotely.

digital – Based on the two binary digits, 1 and 0. The operation of all computers is based on this amazingly simple concept. All forms of information are capable of being digitised – numbers, words, and even sounds and images – and then transmitted over the internet.

directory – On a PC, a folder containing your files.

DNS – Domain name server.

domain name – A name that identifies an IP address. It identifies to the computers on the rest of the internet where to access particular information. Each domain has a name. For someone@somewhere.co.uk, 'somewhere.co.uk' is the domain name.

download – To copy a file from one computer on the internet to your own computer.

ebusiness – The broad concept of doing business to business, and business to consumer sales, over the internet.

ecash – Short for electronic cash.

ecommerce – The various means and techniques of transacting business online.

email – Electronic mail, any message or file you send from your computer to another computer using your 'email client' program (such as Netscape Messenger or Microsoft Outlook).

email address – The unique address given to you by your ISP. It can be used by others using the internet to send email messages to you.

emoticons – Popular symbols used to express emotions in email, for example the well known smiley :-) which means 'I'm smiling!' Emoticons are not normally appropriate for business communications.

encryption – The scrambling of information to make it unreadable without a key or password.

ezines – The term for magazines and newsletters published on the internet.

FAQs – Frequently asked questions.

Favorites – The rather coy term for **bookmarks** used by Internet Explorer, and by America Online.

file – Any body of data such as a word-processed document, a spreadsheet, a database file, a graphics or video file, sound file, or computer program.

filtering software – Software loaded onto a computer to prevent access to unwelcome content on the internet.

firewall – A firewall is special security software designed to stop the flow of certain files into and out of a computer network.

flame – A more or less hostile or aggressive message posted in a newsgroup or to an individual newsgroup user.

folder – The name for a directory on a computer. It is a place in which files are stored.

form – A web page that allows or requires you to enter information into fields on the page and send the information to a web site, program or individual on the web.

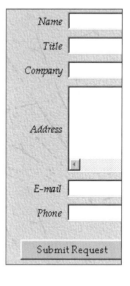

forums – Places for discussion on the internet. They include Usenet newsgroups, mailing lists, and bulletin board services.

frames – A web design feature in which web pages are divided into several areas or panels, each containing separate information.

freespace – An allocation of free web space by an internet service provider or other organisation.

freeware – Software programs made available without charge. Where a small charge is requested, the term is **shareware**.

FTP – File transfer protocol, the method the internet uses to speed files back and forth between computers.

GIF – Graphic interchange format. It is a widely-used compressed file format used on web pages and elsewhere to display files that contain graphic images. See also **JPEG** and **PDF**.

hacker – A person interested in computer programming, operating systems, the internet and computer security. In common usage, the term is often wrongly used to describe crackers.

History list – A record of visited web pages, stored by your browser.

hits – The number of times that items on a web page have been viewed.

home page – The index or main page of a web site.

host – A host is the computer where a particular file or domain is located, and from where people can retrieve it.

HTML – Hyper text markup language, the universal computer language used to create pages on the world wide web.

HTTP – Hypertext transfer protocol, the protocol used by the world wide web.

hyperlink – See **link**.

hypertext – This is a link on an HTML page that, when clicked with a mouse, results in a further HTML page or graphic being loaded into view on your browser.

ICQ – A form of internet chat, derived from the phrase 'I seek you'.

internet – A broad term that encompasses email, web pages, internet chat, newsgroups, mailing lists, bulletin boards, and – video conferencing.

internet2 – A new form of the internet being developed exclusively for educational and academic use.

internet directory – A special web site which consists of categorised information about other web sites. The most widely used is Yahoo! at: http://www.yahoo.com

Internet Explorer – The world's most popular browser software, a product of Microsoft.

Internet protocol number – The numerical code that is a domain name's real address.

internet service providers – Organisations which offer people ('users') access to the internet. The well-known commercial ones in the UK include AOL, CompuServe, BT Internet, Freeserve, Demon and Virgin Net. Services typically include access to the world wide web, email and newsgroups, as well as others such as news, chat, and entertainment.

intranet – Software that uses internet technology to allow communication be-

Glossary of internet terms ....

tween individuals, for example within a large commercial organisation. It often operates on a LAN (local area network).

IP address – An 'internet protocol' address. All computers linked to the internet have one. The address is somewhat like a telephone number, and consists of four sets of numbers separated by dots.

IRC – Internet relay chat. The chat involves typing messages which are sent and read in real time

ISDN – Integrated services digital network, a high-speed telephone network for internet use.

JPEG or **JPG** – The acronym is short for Joint Photographic Experts Group. A JPEG is a specialised file format used to display graphic files on the internet.

kick – To eject someone from a chat channel.

LAN – A local area network, a computer network usually located in one building or campus.

link – A hypertext phrase or image that calls up another web page when you click on it.

LINX – The London Internet Exchange, the facility which maintains UK internet traffic in the UK.

listserver – An automated email system whereby subscribers are able to receive and send email from other subscribers to the list.

lurk – The slang term used to describe reading a newsgroup's messages without actually taking part in that newsgroup. Despite the connotations of the word, it is a perfectly respectable activity on the internet.

macros – 'Macro languages' are used to automate repetitive tasks in Word processors and other applications.

mail server – A remote computer that enables you to send and receive emails.

mailing list – A forum where messages are distributed by email to the members of the forum.

metasearch engine – A site that sends a keyword search to many different search engines and directories so you can use many search engines from one place.

modem – An internal or external piece of hardware plugged into your PC. It links into a standard phone socket, thereby giving you access to the internet. The word derives from MOdulator/DEModulator.

moderator – A person in charge of a mailing list, newsgroup or forum.

MPEG or **MPG** – The file format used for video clips available on the internet. See also JPEG. See http://mpeg.org for further technical information

MP3 – An immensely popular audio format that allows you to download and play music on your computer.

navigate – To click on the hyperlinks on a web site in order to move to other web pages or internet sites.

net – A slang term for the internet. In the same way, the world wide web is often just called the web.

netiquette – Popular term for the unofficial rules and language people follow to keep electronic communication in an acceptably polite form.

Netscape – After Microsoft's Internet Explorer, Netscape Navigator is the most popular browser software for surfing the internet.

newsgroup – A Usenet discussion group. There are 80,000 of them.

newsreader – A type of software that enables you to search, read, post and manage messages in a newsgroup. The best known are Microsoft Outlook, and Netscape Messenger.

news server – A remote computer (e.g. your internet service provider) that enables you to access newsgroups.

nick – Nickname, an alias you can give yourself and use when entering a chat channel, rather than using your real name.

OS – The operating system in a computer, for example MS DOS (Microsoft Disk Operating System), or Windows 95/98.

patch – A small piece of software used to patch up ('fix') a hole or defect ('bug') in a software program.

PC – Personal computer, based on IBM technology. It is distinct from the Apple Macintosh which uses a different operating system

PDA – Personal data assistant – a mobile phone, palm top or any other hand-held processor, typically used to access the internet.

PDF – Portable document format, a handy type of file produced using Adobe Acrobat software. It has universal applications for text and graphics.

PGP – Pretty Good Privacy, a proprietary and highly secure method of encoding a message before transmitting it over the internet.

plug in – A type of (usually free and downloadable) software required to add some form of functionality to web page viewing.

PoP – Point of presence. This refers to the dial-up phone numbers available from your ISP.

portal site – Portal means gateway. It is a web site designed to serve as a general jumping off point into the internet or to some particular part of it.

privacy – To explore internet privacy issues worldwide visit the Electronic Frontier Foundation at www.eff.org, and for the UK, www.netfreedom.org

protocol – Technical term for the method by which computers communicate.

proxy – An intermediate computer or server, used for reasons of security.

Quicktime – A popular free software program from Apple Computers. It is designed to play sounds and images including video clips and animations on both Apple Macs and personal computers.

radio button – A button that, when clicked, looks like this: ◉

refresh, reload – The refresh or reload button on your browser toolbar tells the web page you are looking at to reload.

register – You may have to give your name, personal details and financial information to some sites before you can continue to use the pages.

router – A machine that direct internet data (network packets) from one internet location to another.

script – A script is a set of commands written into the HTML tags of a web page.

scroll, scroll bar – To scroll means to move part of a page or document into view or out of view on the screen. Scrolling is done by using a scroll bar activated by the mouse pointer. Grey scroll bars automatically appear on the right and/or lower edge of the screen if the page contents are too big to fit into view.

search engine – A search engine is a web site you can use for finding something on the internet. The technology variously involves the use of 'bots' (search robots), spiders or crawlers. Popular search engines have developed into big web sites and information centres in their own right. Among the best known are AltaVista, Excite, Infoseek , Lycos, Metasearch and Webcrawler.

secure sockets layer (SSL) – A standard piece of technology which ensures secure financial transactions and data flow over the internet.

server – Any computer on a network that provides access and serves information to other computers.

shareware – Software that you can try before you buy. Usually there is some kind of limitation such as an expiry date.

Shockwave – A popular piece of software produced by Macromedia, which enables you to view animations and other special effects on web sites.

signature file – This is a little text file in which you can place your address details, for adding to email and newsgroup messages.

smiley – A form of **emoticon**.

snail mail – The popular term for the standard postal service involving post-persons, vans, trains, planes, sacks and sorting offices.

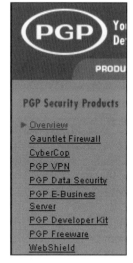

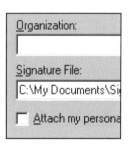

sniffer – A program on a computer system (usually an ISP's system) designed to collect information

spam – Electronic junk mail.

SSL – Secure socket layer, a key part of internet security technology.

subscribe – The term for accessing a newsgroup or internet mailing list in order to read and post messages.

surfing – Slang term for browsing the internet, especially following trails of links on pages across the world wide web.

TCP/IP – Transmission control protocol/internet protocol, the essential technology of the internet.

telnet – Software that allows you to connect via the internet to a remote computer and work as if you were a terminal linked to that system.

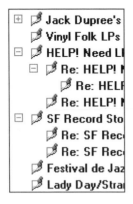

thread – An ongoing topic in a Usenet newsgroup or mailing list discussion. The term refers to the original message on a particular topic, and all the replies and other messages which spin off from it.

thumbnail – A small version of a graphic file which, when clicked, displays a larger version.

top level domain – The last piece of code in a domain name, such as .com or .uk

traffic – The amount of data flowing across the internet, to a particular web site, newsgroup or chat room, or as emails.

trojan horse – A program that seems to perform a useful task but is really a malevolent program designed to cause damage to a computer system.

UNIX – A computer operating system that has been in use for many years, mostly by larger systems.

uploading – The act of copying files from your PC to a server or other PC on the internet, for example when you are publishing your own web pages.

URL – Uniform resource locator, the address of each internet page. For instance the URL of Internet Handbooks is http://www.internet-handbooks.co.uk

Usenet – The collection of some 80,000 active newsgroups that make up a substantial part of the internet.

virtual reality – The presentation of a lifelike scenario in electronic form. It can be used for gaming, business or educational purposes.

virus – A computer program maliciously designed to cause havoc to people's computer files.

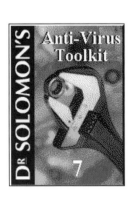

web authoring – Creating HTML pages to upload onto the internet.

web – Short for the world wide web. See **WWW** below.

WAP – Wireless application protocol, new technology that enables mobile phones to access the internet.

webmaster – Any person who manages a web site.

web rings – A network of interlinked web sites that share a common interest.

web site – A set of web pages, owned or managed by the same person or organisation, and which are interconnected by hyperlinks.

Windows – The operating system for personal computers developed by Bill Gates and the Microsoft Corporation. Windows 3.1 was followed by Windows 95, further enhanced by Windows 98. Windows 2000 is the latest.

wizard – A feature of many software programs that guides you through its main stages.

WWW – The world wide web. Since it began in 1994 this has become the most popular part of the internet. The web is now made up of more than a billion web pages of every imaginable description, typically linking to other pages.

WYSIWYG – 'What you see is what you get.' If you see it on the screen, then it should look just the same when you print it out.

Yahoo! – Probably the world's most popular internet directory and search engine.

Index

Index

Building a Web Site on the Internet
A practical guide to writing and commissioning web pages
Brendan Murphy BSc MBA MBSC

The rise in interest in the internet, and especially the word wide web, has been phenomenal. This book meets the urgent need for all business users who need an effective internet presence. Written in plain English, it explains the three main ways of achieving this: create it yourself by writing HTML, create it yourself by using a popular software package, or create it by hiring a web development company. Whether your organisation is large or small, make sure *you* make the right choices for your web site. Brendan Murphy teaches HNC in Computing, and lectures for the Open University (Course T171, You, Your computer and the Net). He is a Member of the British Computer Society, and Institute of Management Information Systems.
1 84025 314 2

Finding a Job on the Internet *2nd edition*
Amazing new possibilities for jobseekers everywhere
Brendan Murphy BSc MBA MBSC

Thinking of looking for a new job, or even a change of career? The internet is a really great place to start your job search. In easy steps and plain English, this practical handbook explains how to find and use internet web sites and newsgroups to give you what you need. School, college and university leavers will find it a valuable resource for identifying suitable employers and getting expert help with CVs and job applications. The book will also be useful for employers thinking of using the internet for recruitment purposes, and for career and training advisers everywhere.
1 84025 365 7 2nd edition

Getting Started on the Internet
A practical step-by-step guide for beginners
Kye Valongo

Confused by search engines, worried about email, baffled by browsers? In plain English, this beginner's guide takes you gently step-by-step through all the basics of the internet. It shows you how to obtain free access to the internet, how to set up your computer, how to look for information, and how to send and receive emails. It explains how to explore newsgroups and internet chat, how to protect your privacy online, and even how to create your own home page. Whether you want the internet for use at home, in education or in the workplace, this is the book for you, specially designed to get you up and running with the minimum fuss and bother.
1 84025 321 5

Internet for Writers
Using the new medium to research, promote and publish your work
Nick Daws BSc(Hons)

This illustrated guide offers all writers with a complete introduction to the internet - how to master the basic skills, and how to use this amazing new medium to create, publish and promote your creative work. Would you like to broaden and speed up your research? Meet fellow writers, editors and publishers through web sites, newsgroups, or chat? Even publish your work on the internet for a potentially enormous new audience? Then this is the book you need, with all the practical starting points to get you going, step by step. The book is a selection of *The UK Good Book Guide*.
1 84025 308 8

Other Internet Handbooks ....

Marketing Your Business on the Internet *2nd edition*
A practical step-by-step guide for all business owners and managers
Sara Edlington

Is your business online? Or perhaps you are still debating whether to take the plunge? For many businesses, the internet will become an essential tool over the next few years. Written by someone experienced in marketing on the internet from its earliest days, this practical book will show you step-by-step how to make a success of marketing your organisation on the internet. Discover how to find a profitable on-line niche, know which ten essential items to have on your web site, how to keep visitors returning again and again, how to secure valuable on- and off-line publicity for your organisation, and how to build your brand online. The internet is set to create phenomenal new marketing opportunities - make sure you win your share.
1 84025 364 9 - 2nd edition

Running a Shop on the Internet
How to set up and run your own profitable online store
Graham Jones BSc (Hons)

Millions of people now shop via the web. This book shows you step-by-step how to set up your own virtual shop on the internet, and win a share of this booming business. It guides you through decisions about which kind of shop to set up, right through to the business and legal issues you need to consider. Find out how to design your online shop for maximum customer appeal. Gain valuable new skills in internet marketing, sales promotion and online payment systems. Explore internet-based customer service systems and methods of distribution. With millions of new consumers coming online, no retailer today can afford to be without this valuable and timely handbook.
1 84025 317 7

Using Credit Cards on the Internet
A practical step-by-step guide for all cardholders and retailers
Graham Jones BSc (Hons)

Are you worried about using credit cards on the internet? Do you know the truth about 'secure transactions'? Would you like to obtain a special online credit card? This valuable new book shows you how to avoid trouble and use your 'virtual plastic' in complete safety over the internet. It contains all the low-down on security, practical tips to make sure that all your credit card dealings are secure, and advice on where to find credit cards with extra 'web protection'. If you are running a business on the internet, it also explains how to set up a 'merchant account' so that customers can safely pay you using their credit cards. The book is complete with a guide to the best sites on credit card usage.
1 84025 349 5

Where to Find It on the Internet - *2nd edition*
Your complete guide to search engines, portals, databases, yellow pages & other internet reference tools
Kye Valongo

Here is a valuable basic reference guide to hundreds of carefully selected web sites for everyone wanting to track down information on the internet. Don't waste time with fruitless searches - get to the sites you want, fast. This book provides a complete selection of the best search engines, online databases, directories, libraries, people finders, yellow pages, portals, and other powerful research tools. A recent selection of 'The Good Book Guide', and now in an updated new edition, this book will be an essential companion for all internet users, whether at home, in education, or in the workplace.
1 84025 369 X - 2nd edition